REMEMBER

MEMORIES

BIOGRAPHY

TRADITIONS

CULTURE

HERITAGE

happy holidays and new year....

MIAMI

MAY

1996

FLORIDA

BETTER SCRAPBOOKING

VANESSA-ANN

Sterling Publishing Co., Inc. New York
A Sterling / Chapelle Book

CHAPELLE:
- JO PACKHAM, OWNER
- CATHY SEXTON, EDITOR
- STAFF: MARIE BARBER, ANN BEAR, ARETA BINGHAM, KASS BURCHETT, REBECCA CHRISTENSEN, BRENDA DONCOUSE, DANA DURNEY, HOLLY FULLER, MARILYN GOFF, AMBER HANSEN, HOLLY HOLLINGSWORTH, SUSAN JORGENSEN, BARBARA MILBURN, LINDA ORTON, JAMIE PIERCE, KARMEN QUINNEY, LESLIE RIDENOUR, CINDY STOECKL, AND GINA SWAPP

PHOTOGRAPHY:
- KEVIN DILLEY, PHOTOGRAPHER FOR HAZEN PHOTOGRAPHY

If you have any questions or comments, please contact Chapelle, Ltd., Inc., P.O. Box 9252, Ogden, UT 84409 • (801) 621-2777 • (801) 621-2788 Fax • e-mail: Chapelle1@aol.com

The written instructions, photographs, designs, patterns, and projects in this volume are intended for the personal use of the reader and may be reproduced for that purpose only. Any other use, especially commercial use, is forbidden under law without the written permission of the copyright holder. Every effort has been made to ensure that all the information in this book is accurate. However, due to differing conditions, tools, and individual skills, the publisher cannot be responsible for any injuries, losses, and other damages which may result from the use of the information in this book.

If rubber cement is not available in your area, consult with any local crafts store to find a comparable product.

Library of Congress Cataloging-in-Publication Data

Vanessa-Ann.
    Better scrapbooking / Vanessa-Ann.
        p.   cm.
    "A Sterling/Chapelle book."
    Includes index.
    ISBN 0-8069-6465-0
    1. Photograph albums.   2. Photographs--Conservation and restoration.   3. Scrapbooks.   I. Title.
    TR465.V357   1999   99-23778
    771'.46--dc21   CIP

10 9 8 7 6 5 4 3 2 1

Published by Sterling Publishing Company, Inc.
387 Park Avenue South, New York, NY 10016
© 1999 by Chapelle Ltd.
Distributed in Canada by Sterling Publishing
c/o Canadian Manda Group, One Atlantic Avenue, Suite 105
Toronto, Ontario, Canada M6K 3E7
Distributed in Great Britain and Europe by Cassell PLC
Wellington House, 125 Strand, London WC2R 0BB, England
Distributed in Australia by Capricorn Link (Australia) Pty Ltd.
P.O. Box 6651, Baulkham Hills, Business Centre, NSW 2153, Australia
Printed and Bound in China
All Rights Reserved

Sterling ISBN 0-8069-6465-0

CONTENTS

INTRODUCTION

In recent months, scrapbooking has become one of the most popular pasttimes. There are several books available on the basics that give general scrapbooking information. The concept of this book was to take scrapbooking to a new level.

Everyone has artistic talent that helps define them as individuals. For those of you who have already mastered the techniques described in this book, your scrapbook pages will come easily. Our hope is that this book will help those who might not know where their talents lie, find a crafting technique that is suited to their abilities and personalities. We know that they too can create scrapbook pages with artistic flair, without spending unreasonable amounts of time.

The secret is to spend less time scrapbooking, and more time making the memories that we would want to scrapbook. Our memories provide us the ability to reflect back over the course of our lives and to remember moments that we wish we could re-live. It is okay to spend a little extra time to create the first page in your scrapbook as this will probably set the theme for the entire album. However, since we all have limited time to spend putting our scrapbooks together, the subsequent pages in the album should be kept simpler and the time spent on them should be kept to a minimum. Border pages serve this purpose well. One alternative for having every page in your scrapbook look as though you spent hours on it is to create that one special page and have it color-copied to make several background pages.

Most scrapbooking experts recommend using only scrapbooking products and techniques that have been proven to be archival. Unfortunately, we are unable to guarantee that the techniques described in this book, including the products used, are archival. We can, however, guarantee that using these simple ideas will render incredible results and your scrapbook will be as individual and unique as you. Your scrapbook will be one that your posterity will cherish, not only because of the photos you have preserved, but because you have included your own personal artistic self in each and every page.

CHOOSING AN APPROPRIATE ADHESIVE

There are several adhesives available that serve the same basic purpose. The type of adhesive that you choose should be based on personal preference, availability, and the project being created.

• Spray Adhesive:
Spray adhesive comes in a can and is considered permanent. Once the photo, cut-out, die-cut, stenciled motif, etc., is mounted on the background page it cannot be removed.

• Glue Pen:
Glue pens have various styles of tip applicators, which make them ideal when working with specific sized photos and artwork. Glue pens dispense a tacky glue that is easy to reposition when necessary.

• Tape and Double-sided Tabs:
Tape and double-sided tabs are best used with heavier papers because lightweight papers taped together might have a ridge from the tape.

• Glue Stick:
Glue sticks are readily available and are considered archival. Care must be taken when using them to avoid smears and smudges.

• Rubber Cement:
Rubber cement is a popular adhesive because the excess can be "rolled" into a ball and comes off the page easily.

• Adhesive Application Machine:
This machine allows an adhesive backing to be applied to any piece of paper or card stock.

FAMILY

HEIRLOOM

HISTORY

ANCESTORS

POSTERITY

"AT TIMES I CAN ALMOST FEEL THE PRESENCE
OF MY ANCESTORS — A GENTLE, GUIDING TOUCH
FROM THOSE WHO'VE GONE BEFORE."
— AUTHOR UNKNOWN

DÉCOUPAGING

1 Gather vintage photos, letters, postcards, telegrams, and relics from ancestors — keys, jewelry, hair combs, badges, watches, pens, etc. Things that lie flat work best.

2 Arrange the relics as desired on the glass of a color copy machine. Carefully place one or more old letters over the relics, then gently close the lid on the copy machine. Make a copy. The copy should have colors in shadows rather than in gray tones. It may be necessary to "trick" the copy machine by placing a colored piece of self-adhesive paper along the edge of one of the letters. This will cause the machine to read "color" instead of "black and white." All copies may be reduced or enlarged and cut to the dimensions of the pages in the purchased scrapbook album. Make several different page layouts or make multiples of the same page to be used as the background pages.

3 Make a copy of vintage photos, either in color or in black and white. These photos may be reduced or enlarged and the color copies cropped to accommodate the configuration of the page layout. If desired, use decorative-edged scissors to trim the color copies.

4 Using a ½" flat paintbrush and découpage medium, découpage the copied background pages to the album pages. Once the photos have been cropped to the desired shapes and sizes, découpage them to the background pages. Using a rubber brayer, remove the air pockets; then wipe off any excess découpage medium. Let the découpage medium dry thoroughly. Protect the pages with waxed paper and press under a heavy book or other weight for 12 to 24 hours.

BASIC SUPPLIES: Heavy book or other weight; rubber brayer; découpage medium (matte finish); letters; ½" flat paintbrush; vintage photos; postcards; relics from ancestors; scissors; purchased scrapbook album with pages included; telegrams; photo cropping templates; waxed paper

ADDITIONAL SUPPLIES: Craft knife; cutting mat; jute; decorative-edged scissors

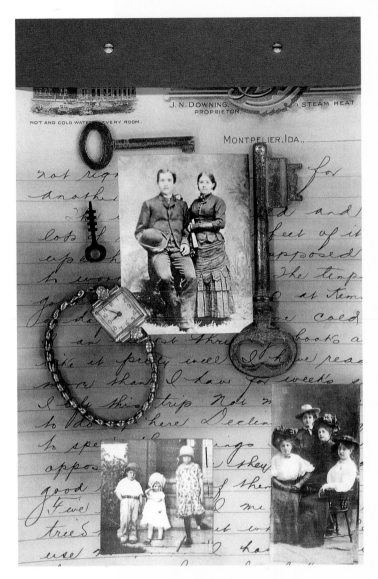

1 Make copies of relics on a color copy machine to create the background pages. Make copies of vintage photos to be used.

2 Découpage the copied background pages to the album pages; then découpage the photos in place as desired.

3 Using a sharp craft knife, trim some of the cropped photos around the copied relics so the photos appear to be placed behind or underneath the treasured items. As shown above, the photos have been trimmed around the configurations of the watch and key and around the configurations of the locket and heart pin.

4 Using a rubber brayer, remove the air pockets; then wipe off any excess découpage medium. Let the découpage medium dry thoroughly. Press under a heavy book to prevent curling.

"WE DO NOT REMEMBER DAYS,
WE REMEMBER MOMENTS."
— CESARE PAVESE

1 Make copies of relics on a color copy machine to create the background pages. Make copies of the vintage photos to be used.

2 Découpage the copied background pages to the album pages; then découpage the photos in place as desired.

3 Make a color copy of vintage postcards (address and stamped side down) reduced to 50% of original size. Cut out the copied postcards and tie jute around each one. As shown above, place the postcards on top of the photos that have been placed and trimmed along the outside edges of the background pages. Découpage the postcards in place.

4 Using a rubber brayer, remove the air pockets; then wipe off any excess découpage medium. Let the découpage medium dry thoroughly. Press under a heavy book to prevent curling.

"THE MOST TREASURED HEIRLOOMS
ARE THE SWEET MEMORIES OUR FAMILIES HAVE BESTOWED UPON US."
— AUTHOR UNKNOWN

EMBELLISHING & BINDING THE COVER

Disassemble a purchased scrapbook album. Cut a piece of linen fabric to the dimensions necessary to cover the album, allowing at least one inch on all sides for folding over to the inside of the album. Place the linen fabric, right side down, on a clean, flat surface that has been covered with waxed paper to protect it.

Using a 1/2" flat paintbrush, apply découpage medium over the outside cover of the album. It may be necessary to do this one section at a time. Center the album over the linen fabric and press down to remove air pockets. Bring the edges of the linen fabric around to the inside of the album cover and adhere with découpage medium. To reduce bulk, clip and miter the corners. Let the découpage medium dry thoroughly.

Using a hot-glue gun, adhere a piece of metallic trim around the cover as shown, securing the ends on the inside as with the linen fabric.

Using découpage medium, adhere extra photocopies of the background pages that have been cut to fit to the inside of the album cover to hide the raw edges of the linen fabric and metallic trim. This is a fun way to create a theme, beginning with the scrapbook album cover and continuing throughout the album pages.

Use color copies of small vintage photos (or photos reduced in size) to embellish the tops of decorative antique buttons. Crop the photos to fit and adhere in place with découpage medium. Using a hot-glue gun, adhere the buttons to the front of the album.

Tie a piece of black lace around the front cover of the album near the spine. Place a knot in the lace on the right side and cut the ends of the lace at an angle.

Thread a large needle with jute. Place the completed scrapbook pages in the desired order and place them inside the album cover. Insert the needle through the existing hole in the back of the album cover, up through all of the pages, and out through the front of the cover. Pull the jute, leaving about seven inches at the back of the album. Insert the needle through the remaining hole in the front of the album cover, down through all of the pages, and out through the back of the cover. Remove the needle and tie the ends of the jute into a bow. If necessary, trim the ends. This will bind the book and secure all the pages inside the purchased scrapbook album.

Photo shown on page 8.

SUPPLIES FOR EMBELLISHING THE COVER:
Decorative antique buttons with smooth center sections; color copies of vintage photos; découpage medium (matte finish); linen fabric; hot-glue gun and glue sticks; jute; black lace; measuring tape; large needle; 1/2" flat paintbrush; extra photocopies of the background pages; scissors; purchased scrapbook album with pages included; metallic trim; waxed paper

WEDDING
VOWS

LOVE

ROMANCE

HONEYMOON

"THE LOVE IN OUR FAMILY FLOWS STRONG AND DEEP,
LEAVING US MEMORIES TO TREASURE AND KEEP."
—AUTHOR UNKNOWN

EMBOSSING & GOLD LEAFING

1 Embossing is the technique used to achieve dimensional pages that, visually and to the touch, have raised surface areas. Place the photocopy or card stock face down on a light box. Using an embossing tool, emboss the image(s) by rubbing over the edges and the larger solid areas. If the embossing does not appear raised enough, place a scrap piece of white velvet over the light box to provide cushioning. Using white velvet will allow you to see through it.

2 Gold leafing is the technique used to accent special areas of an image with actual gold leaf. Using a $1/2$" flat paintbrush, apply gold leaf adhesive to all of the areas that will be gold leafed. Let the gold leaf adhesive dry thoroughly. Clean the paintbrush with soapy water. Apply the gold leafing to all of the prepared areas according to the manufacturer's directions. Using a soft dry brush, remove any excess gold leafing.

3 Make a copy of chosen photos, either in color or in black and white. These photos may be reduced or enlarged and the color copies cropped to accommodate the configuration of the page layout. If desired, use decorative-edged scissors to trim the color copies.

4 Once the photos have been cropped to the desired shapes and sizes, adhere them to the back of the wallpaper, embossed photocopy, or embossed card stock. If embossing was not used, the photos can be adhered directly to the album pages. Using an appropriate adhesive, adhere the wallpaper, embossed, and/or gold leafed background pages to the album pages. Protect the pages with waxed paper and press under a heavy book or other weight for 12 to 24 hours.

BASIC SUPPLIES: Adhesive; heavy book or other weight; soft dry brush; parchment card stock; embossing tool; gold leaf adhesive; gold leafing; assortment of lace and trims; light box; measuring tape; $1/8$" and $1/2$" flat paintbrushes; journaling pen or marker; photos; scissors; purchased scrapbook album with pages included; photo cropping templates; scrap piece of white velvet; waxed paper

ADDITIONAL SUPPLIES: Assortment of card stock; gold-foiled paper lace corners; craft knife; cutting mat; découpage medium (matte finish); matches; acrylic paints; pencil; decorative-edged ruler; decorative-edged scissors; sponge; metal stamp; decorative stencil; heart-shaped template; white embossed wallpaper; gold sealing wax stick

1 Find a white embossed wallpaper that has an appropriate area to cut out for the placement of a photo. Cut the wallpaper to the dimensions of the pages in the purchased scrapbook album.

2 Using a sharp craft knife, cut a "window" in the wallpaper for the photo. Using an appropriate adhesive, adhere the photo to the back of the wallpaper, positioning the photo in the window as desired.

3 Adhere the wallpaper to the album page.

4 Place one gold-foiled paper lace corner in opposite corners of each background page.

1 Cut a piece of white lace to fit horizontally across the pages in the purchased scrapbook album. Cut a piece of white lace to fit vertically down the pages.

2 Temporarily adhere the pieces of lace to a piece of parchment card stock.

3 Cut ¹/₂" scalloped lace into a rectangular shape for the photo "window," miter each corner, and adhere in place on the parchment card stock as desired.

4 Make copies on a color copy machine in black-and-white mode. Cut the photocopies to the dimensions of the pages in the purchased scrapbook album.

5 Place one photocopy at a time face down on a light box. Using an embossing tool, emboss the lace by rubbing over the edges and the larger solid areas.

6 Using a sharp craft knife, cut the center from the "lace window" on the embossed photocopy for the photo. Using an appropriate adhesive, adhere the photo to the back of the embossed photocopy, positioning the photo in the window as desired.

7 Adhere the embossed photocopy to the album page.

8 As shown above, cut pieces of gold trim to fit vertically down the album pages (two per page). Adhere the gold trim to the pages, over the embossed lace.

1 Place the eyelet lace on waxed paper. Using a 1/2" flat paintbrush, apply découpage medium onto the lace to seal it. Make certain to keep all "openings" in the lace open. Let the découpage medium dry thoroughly. Clean the paintbrush with water.

2 Using the clean paintbrush, apply gold leaf adhesive to the pieces of sealed lace. Let the gold leaf adhesive dry thoroughly. Clean the paintbrush with soapy water. Apply the gold leafing to the lace according to the manufacturer's directions. Using a soft dry brush, remove any excess gold leafing.

1 Cut pieces of eyelet lace to fit across the tops of the pages in the purchased scrapbook album. Place the pieces of eyelet lace on waxed paper.

2 Using a ½" flat paintbrush, apply découpage medium onto the lace to seal it. Make certain to keep all "openings" in the lace open. Let the découpage medium dry thoroughly. Clean the paintbrush with water.

3 Using the clean paintbrush, apply gold leaf adhesive to the pieces of sealed lace. Let the gold leaf adhesive dry thoroughly. Clean the paintbrush with soapy water. As shown above, apply the gold leafing to the lace according to the manufacturer's directions. Using a soft dry brush, remove any excess gold leafing.

4 Cut pieces of gold trim to fit across the bottoms of the pages.

5 As shown above, the album page can be sponged with metallic gold acrylic paint to accent it.

6 Using an appropriate adhesive, adhere the lace to the tops and the gold trim to the bottoms of the album pages.

7 Adhere the photos in place and add pieces of gold trim in the opposite corners of each photo.

8 Press under a heavy book to prevent curling.

1 Temporarily adhere the doilies to a piece of parchment card stock. Place the parchment card stock and the doilies face down on a light box.

2 Using an embossing tool, emboss only the openings of the doilies by rubbing over the edges and the larger solid areas.

1 To emboss velvet, place a tatted doily on an ironing board. Heat the iron to the "cotton" setting. Place one piece of velvet, right side down, over the doily and dampen with a spray bottle.

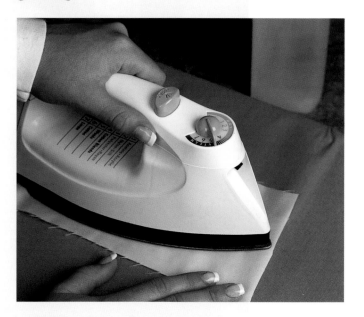

2 Place the iron on the fabric, using pressure, but no movement. Pick up the iron, place the iron on a new section of the fabric, and repeat until the design of the doily is complete. Be careful not to scorch the velvet.

1 Find a couple of tatted doilies that are small enough to fit within the dimensions of the pages in the purchased scrapbook album. Overlap the doilies to add interest. Temporarily adhere the doilies to a piece of parchment card stock.

2 Place the parchment card stock and the doilies face down on a light box. Using an embossing tool, emboss only the openings of the doilies by rubbing over the edges and the larger solid areas.

3 Using a sharp craft knife, cut the centers from the embossed doilies on the card stock to make "windows" for the photos. Using an appro-

priate adhesive, adhere the photos to the back of the embossed card stock, positioning the photos in the windows as desired.

4 Adhere the embossed card stock to the album page. As shown above, adhere one of the "removed centers" to the corner of the page for additional accent.

5 Using a 1/2" flat paintbrush, apply gold leaf adhesive to all of the embossed areas. Let the gold leaf adhesive dry thoroughly. Clean the paintbrush with soapy water. As shown above, apply the gold leafing according to the manufacturer's directions. Using a soft dry brush, remove any excess gold leafing.

1 Find a piece of white lace that is large enough to cover the dimensions of the pages in the purchased scrapbook album.

2 Temporarily adhere the lace to a piece of parchment card stock.

3 Make copies on a color copy machine in black-and-white mode. Cut the photocopies to the dimensions of the pages in the purchased scrapbook album.

4 Place one photocopy at a time face down on a light box. Using an embossing tool, emboss the lace by rubbing over the edges and the larger solid areas.

5 Using a heart-shaped template and a sharp craft knife, cut heart-shaped "windows" on the embossed photocopy for the photos. Using an appropriate adhesive, adhere the photos to the back of the embossed photocopy, positioning the photos in the windows as desired.

6 Adhere the embossed photocopy to the album page.

7 Using a $1/8$" flat paintbrush, apply a border of gold leaf adhesive around each heart. Let the gold leaf adhesive dry thoroughly. Clean the paintbrush with soapy water. As shown above, apply the gold leafing around each heart according to the manufacturer's directions. Using a soft dry brush, remove any excess gold leafing.

1 Cut card stock to the dimensions of the pages in the purchased scrapbook album.

2 As shown above, the album page can be sponged with metallic gold acrylic paint to accent it.

3 Place a decorative stencil on a light box. Position the card stock right side down over the stencil.

4 Using an embossing tool, emboss the openings of the stencil by rubbing over the edges and the larger solid areas.

5 Using a sharp craft knife, cut a "window" in the card stock for the photo. Using an appropriate adhesive, adhere the photo to the back of the card stock, positioning the photo in the window as desired.

6 Adhere the card stock to the album page.

7 Using a $1/8$" flat paintbrush, apply gold leaf adhesive to all of the embossed areas. Let the gold leaf adhesive dry thoroughly. Clean the paintbrush with soapy water. As shown above, apply the gold leafing according to the manufacturer's directions. Using a soft dry brush, remove any excess gold leafing.

8 As shown above, cut pieces of gold trim to fit around the photo. Adhere the gold trim in place.

1 Cut a piece of white card stock to the dimensions of the pages in the purchased scrapbook album. Using a pencil and decorative-edged ruler, trace the design diagonally onto the card stock.

2 Cut along the traced lines.

3 Turn the decorative-edged ruler in the opposite direction, place it approximately 1½" from the cut edge, and trace as before.

4 Place card stock on a light box. Using an embossing tool, emboss along the traced line.

5 Using a ⅛" flat paintbrush, apply gold leaf adhesive along the embossed line. Let the gold leaf adhesive dry thoroughly. Clean the paintbrush with soapy water. As shown above, apply the gold leafing according to the manufacturer's directions. Using a soft dry brush, remove any excess gold leafing.

6 As shown above, the album page can be sponged with metallic gold acrylic paint to accent it.

7 As shown above, trim one corner of the card stock at an angle. Adhere the card stock to the album page to create a "pocket."

8 Using a match, light a gold sealing wax stick and drip wax onto the upper left-hand corner of the card stock in the shape of a heart. Press a metal stamp into the center of the wax. The wax will harden as it cools.

9 Finally, slide the photo(s) into the pocket.

EMBELLISHING & BINDING THE COVER

1 Disassemble a purchased scrapbook album. Remove the spine. Using a 1/2" flat paintbrush, apply gold leaf adhesive to completely cover the outside of the spine. Let the gold leaf adhesive dry thoroughly. Clean the paintbrush with soapy water. Apply sheets of gold leafing to cover the spine according to the manufacturer's directions. Using a soft dry brush, remove any excess gold leafing.

2 Cut a piece of velvet to the dimensions necessary to cover the front and the back of the album, allowing at least one inch on all sides for folding over to the inside of the album. To emboss the pieces of velvet, place a tatted doily on an ironing board as shown on page 22. Heat the iron to the "cotton" setting. Place one piece of velvet, right side down, over the doily and dampen with a spray bottle. Place the iron on the fabric, using pressure, but no movement. Pick up the iron, place the iron on a new section of the fabric, and repeat until the design of the doily is complete. Be careful not to scorch the velvet. Repeat the process on the remaining piece of velvet.

3 Using a hot-glue gun, adhere cotton batting to the front and the back of the album cover. Place the embossed velvet, right side down, on a clean, flat surface that has been covered with waxed paper to protect it. Center the front of the album over the embossed velvet. Bring the edges of the embossed vel-

vet around to the inside of the album cover and adhere with hot glue. To reduce bulk, clip and miter the corners. Repeat the process to cover the back of the album.

4 Using a hot-glue gun, adhere embossed wallpaper (or parchment card stock) that has been cut to fit the inside of the album cover to hide the raw edges of the embossed velvet. This is a fun way to create a theme, beginning with the scrapbook album cover and continuing throughout the album pages.

5 Using a hot-glue gun, adhere braided trim around the front of the album cover, except for the left-hand side (spine edge). Repeat the process around the back of the album cover, except for the right-hand side (spine edge).

6 Place the completed scrapbook pages in the desired order and place them inside the album cover. Reassemble the purchased scrapbook album, replacing the spine.

7 Using a hot-glue gun, adhere small gold tassels to the ends of a twenty inch length of braided trim that has been knotted at each end. Fold the braided trim in half and tie a knot near the bottom to connect the two strands. Adhere the top of the braided trim to the top left-hand side of the scrapbook album.

Photo shown on page 16.

SUPPLIES FOR EMBELLISHING THE COVER: Cotton batting; soft dry brush; tatted doily; hot-glue gun and glue sticks; gold leaf adhesive; gold leafing; iron and ironing board; 1/2" flat paintbrush; scissors; purchased scrapbook album with pages included; spray bottle; small gold tassels; braided trim; velvet; embossed wallpaper or parchment card stock; waxed paper

NATURE
NATURE
ADVENTURE
EXPLORE
THE GREAT OUTDOORS
WILDERNESS

"THE GOAL OF LIFE IS LIVING IN AGREEMENT WITH NATURE."
— ZENO

RUBBER STAMPING

1 The actual scrapbook album shown in this section is not one that has been purchased. Cut the pages for this album from an assortment of colored card stock in a random, freeform style. No pattern is necessary, any shape that is desired can be cut. The only rule is to make certain to leave the left-hand side of each sheet straight so the scrapbook album can be neatly bound. The number of pages is also optional.

2 Embellish each page in the scrapbook album with a variety of rubber stamping techniques. If the album has a theme, make certain to carry that theme throughout. This is easily achieved by using coordinating or contrasting color combinations and alternating them from page to page.

3 Once the photos have been cropped to the desired shapes and sizes, adhere them directly to the background pages or to card stock for matting. As desired, the photos can be single- or double-matted and trimmed with decorative-edged scissors. For an intriguing way to continue the theme, embellish the photo mats with a variety of rubber stamping techniques as with the background pages.

BASIC SUPPLIES: Adhesive; rubber brayer; assortment of card stock; journaling pen or marker; photos; pigment inks; rubber cement; assortment of rubber stamps; scissors; raised stamp pads; photo cropping templates

ADDITIONAL SUPPLIES: Embossing fluid; embossing fluid pen; assortment of embossing powders; embossing tape; acrylic glazes; heat tool; disposable palette; photo corners; decorative-edged scissors; small sponge; assortment of sponge stamps; cardboard squeegee

"CHILDREN NEED ADULTS WHO CAN GO FOR CASUAL WALKS
AND TALK ABOUT FISHING AND STUFF LIKE THAT ...
AND SLOW DOWN TO LOOK AT PRETTY LEAVES AND CATERPILLARS ...
AND ANSWER QUESTIONS ABOUT GOD
AND THE NATURE OF THE WORLD AS IT IS."
— AUTHOR UNKNOWN

1 Cut the background page from terra-cotta card stock.

2 Using rubber cement, randomly brush the adhesive in a "splish-splash" motion over the background page. Do not cover all of the card stock; leave some areas exposed. Let the rubber cement dry thoroughly.

3 Using a small raised stamp pad with dark brown pigment ink, blot it over the entire background page. Let the ink dry thoroughly, then rub the rubber cement off the page.

4 Using a simple patterned block rubber stamp with olive green ink, randomly stamp the background page. Using a large postage stamp rubber stamp with dark brown ink, randomly stamp the background page.

5 Using postage stamp-edged scissors, cut the photo mats from lighter terra-cotta card stock. Repeat random stamping on the photo mats as with the background page.

6 Using an appropriate adhesive, adhere the photos to the stamped photo mats, then adhere the matted photos in place as desired.

1 Cut the background page from olive green card stock.

2 Load ink on a rubber brayer by rolling it over a large raised stamp pad with autumn colored pigment inks. Roll the brayer back and forth over the stamp pad numerous times. Roll it diagonally over the entire background page. Let the ink dry thoroughly.

3 Using a dancing kokopelli rubber stamp with terra-cotta ink, randomly stamp the contour of the bottom of the background page.

4 Cut a 1"-wide freeform strip from terra-cotta card stock.

5 Using a small raised stamp pad with dark brown pigment ink, blot it over the entire freeform strip. Let the ink dry thoroughly, then adhere it to the background page near the bottom. Make certain to apply the adhesive just along the bottom edge of the freeform strip so the photos can be tucked behind it as shown above.

6 Using an appropriate adhesive, adhere the photos in place as desired.

1 Cut the background page from dark tan card stock.

2 Using a zebra stripe block rubber stamp with tan ink, randomly stamp the background page. Using a polka-dot block rubber stamp with white ink, randomly stamp the background page.

3 To border the background page, apply embossing tape across the top, down the right-hand side, and across the bottom of the background page, overlapping in the corners. Generously cover the embossing tape with copper embossing powder; then remove any excess embossing powder (do not discard it as it can be reused). Using a heat tool, emboss the border on the page.

4 Using a postage stamp rubber stamp with embossing fluid, stamp one image onto copper card stock. Emboss as with embossing tape border. Cut out the embossed image leaving a 1/8" border.

5 Using deckle-edged scissors, cut photo frames from the copper card stock in unusual shapes. As shown above, one photo frame was created from four strips of card stock.

6 Using the zebra stripe block and polka-dot block rubber stamps, repeat random stamping on the photo frames as with the background page.

7 Using an appropriate adhesive, adhere the photos behind the stamped photo frames, then adhere the framed photos in place as desired.

8 Adhere the embossed postage stamp image to the lower right-hand corner of the background page.

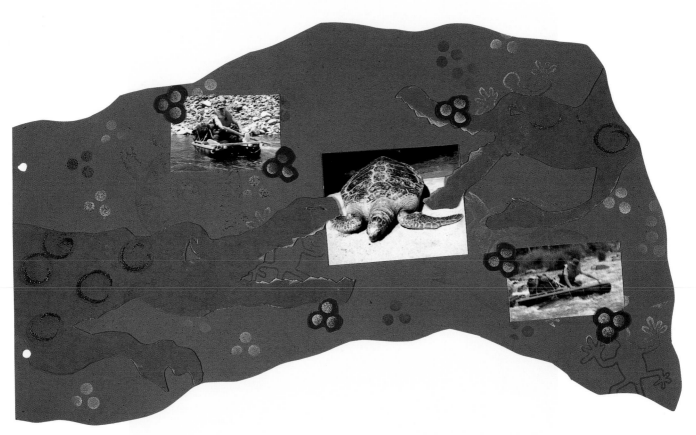

1 Cut the background page from copper card stock.

2 Using a three dot sponge stamp with white ink, randomly stamp the background page. Stamp several additional images onto dark brown card stock to be used as photo corners. Cut out the stamped images leaving a $1/8$" border.

3 Using the same sponge stamp with dark brown ink, randomly stamp the background page.

4 Using a lizard rubber stamp with white ink on the top half and burgundy ink on the bottom half, randomly stamp the background page.

5 Cut two freeform crocodiles from olive green card stock.

6 Using an embossing fluid pen, draw small coils on the crocodiles. Generously cover the embossing fluid with clear embossing powder, then remove any excess embossing powder (do not discard it as it can be reused). Using a heat tool, emboss the coils.

7 Using a small star rubber stamp with dark yellow ink, randomly stamp the crocodiles. Using a small sponge with white ink, dab the crocodiles' teeth.

8 Using an appropriate adhesive, adhere the photos in place as desired.

9 Adhere the crocodiles in place and add one stamped photo corner in opposite corners of each photo.

1 Cut the background page from light terra-cotta card stock.

2 Using a multispiral block rubber stamp with white ink, randomly stamp the background page, overlapping as desired.

3 Using a large single-spiral rubber stamp with embossing fluid, randomly stamp the background page, over the stamped spiral clusters, with five or six images. Generously cover the embossing fluid with clear embossing powder; then remove any excess embossing powder (do not discard it as it can be reused). Using a heat tool, emboss the large spirals.

4 Cut a freeform photo frame from the light terra-cotta card stock.

5 Using the multispiral block rubber stamp, repeat random stamping on the photo frame as with the background page.

6 Using small and medium single-spiral rubber stamps, repeat random stamping and embossing on the photo frame as with the background page.

7 Using an appropriate adhesive, adhere the photo behind the stamped photo frame, then mat the photo frame with terra-cotta card stock. Adhere the framed photo in place as desired.

"GOD DOES NOT DEDUCT
FROM MAN'S LIFE
THE TIME SPENT FISHING."
— AUTHOR UNKNOWN

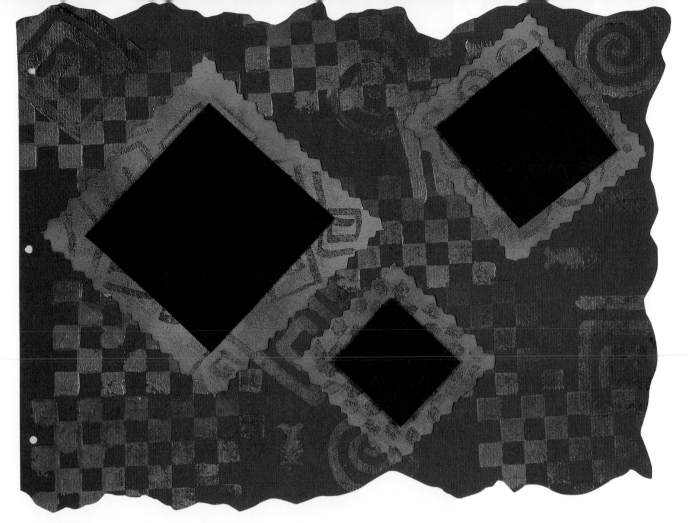

1 Cut the background page from dark brown card stock.

2 Squeeze a two-inch line of gold acrylic glaze onto a disposable palette. Next to it, squeeze a two-inch line of terra-cotta acrylic glaze. Using a squeegee, made from a piece of cardboard, spread the glazes into a fairly thin layer. Make certain not to get the layer too thin or the glaze will not stick to the rubber stamps. It is important to use acrylic glaze because it dries slower than acrylic paint. If it is necessary to use acrylic paint, make certain to add a liquid extender to your mixture.

3 Using a large checkerboard sponge stamp with the glaze mixture, randomly stamp the background page. Using large single-spiral, large square spiral, and small fish skeleton rubber stamps with the glaze mixture, randomly stamp the background page, overlapping checkerboard images as desired.

4 Using peak-edged scissors, cut the photo mats from dark tan card stock.

5 Using an embossing fluid pen, randomly draw spirals and checks on the photo mats. Generously cover the embossing fluid with gold embossing powder; then remove any excess embossing powder (do not discard it as it can be reused). Using a heat tool, emboss the images.

6 Using an appropriate adhesive, adhere the photos to the embossed photo mats, then adhere the matted photos in place as desired.

1 Cut the background page from off-white card stock.

2 Apply embossing fluid over the entire background page. Generously cover the embossing fluid with gold, copper, and clear embossing powders; then remove any excess embossing powder (do not discard it as it can be reused, but put it into a separate container since the colors will now be mixed). Using a heat tool, emboss the entire background page.

3 Using a small fish skeleton rubber stamp with embossing fluid, randomly stamp a stream of fish diagonally across the background page. Emboss as with background page, but this time use only brick red embossing powder.

4 Using an appropriate adhesive and gold photo corners, adhere the photos in place as desired. Because of the heavy texture on the background page, it may be necessary to use some additional adhesive.

EMBELLISHING & BINDING THE COVER

1 The slip cover for this scrapbook album must be assembled after the scrapbook has been made so the slip cover is the correct size to fit all of the freeform pages.

2 Using handmade paper to color coordinate with the background pages within the scrapbook album, fold into an envelope that will adequately accommodate the album pages. Make certain to leave no raw edges. Refer to the diagram below.

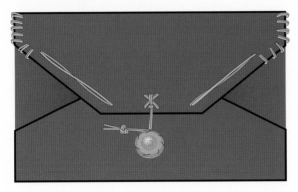

3 If desired, randomly stamp various images over the entire envelope with an ink color that is slightly darker than the color of the handmade paper.

4 Using a large-eyed needle and jute, sew around the edges of the upper flap on the envelope. Tie off the jute in the back with a simple knot.

5 Using an appropriate adhesive, adhere a large flat button to the center of the bottom flap on the envelope. If preferred, the button can be sewn in place.

6 Sew an "X" in the center of the point on the envelope and tie a loop of jute to it. This loop must be long enough to wrap around the button for closing the slip cover.

7 Using a preformed wax seal and a heat tool, melt the wax onto the top of the button. Press a medium spiral rubber stamp into the center of the wax. The wax will harden as it cools.

8 Using a 1/8" paper punch, punch three holes on the left-hand side of each page so the pages line up as desired. Thread a large-eyed needle with jute. Place the completed scrapbook pages in the desired order. Insert the needle through each of the punched holes, one at a time, going through all of the album pages, and tie with a simple knot. Leave enough slack so pages open easily. This will bind the book and secure all the pages inside the album. The album will then be stored in the slip cover (envelope).

Photo shown on page 28.

SUPPLIES FOR EMBELLISHING THE COVER: Adhesive; large flat button; heat tool; large-eyed needle; jute; handmade paper; 1/8" paper punch; assortment of rubber stamps; scissors; assortment of colored stamp pads; preformed wax seal

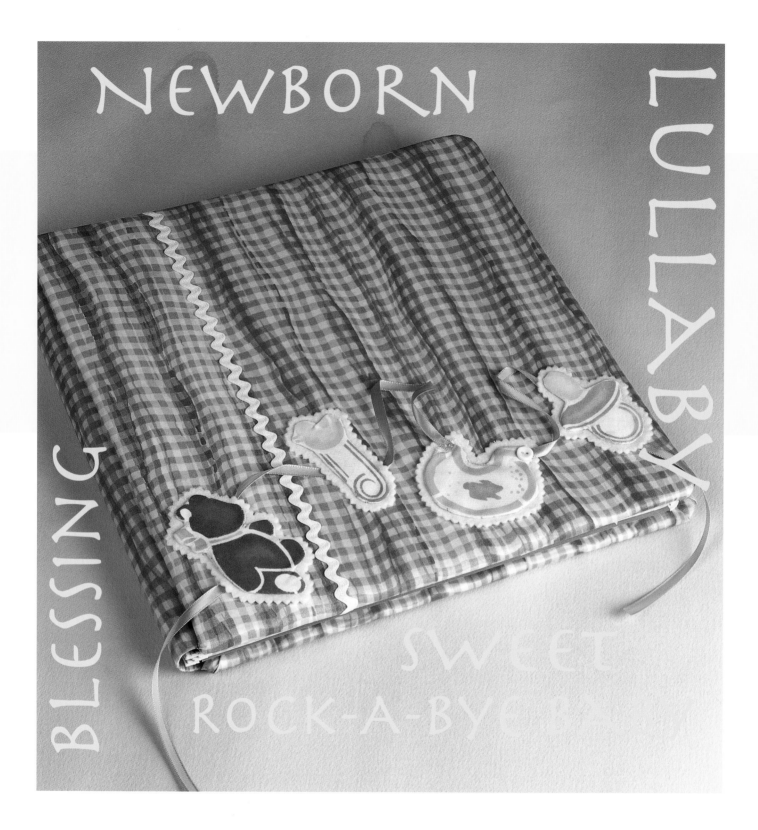

BLESSING

SWEET ROCK-A-BYE BABY

"A BABY IS A GIFT FROM ABOVE — ONE TO CHERISH, ONE TO LOVE."
—AUTHOR UNKNOWN

STENCILING

1 Choose solid or patterned papers to be used as the background pages. Using an appropriate adhesive, adhere the chosen background pages to the album pages.

2 Using decorative stencils, acrylic paints, and a makeup wedge sponge, stencil all of the chosen motifs onto white card stock. Cut out the stenciled motifs and mat as desired. Matting helps to add dimension. The stenciled motifs can be matted with a single mat or a double mat from solid or patterned papers or a combination of each. A small border of $1/8$" makes a nice simple accent to any motif and larger borders up to $1/2$" are nice when using larger images.

3 Once the photos have been cropped to the desired shapes and sizes, adhere them directly to the background pages or to card stock for matting. As desired, the photos can be single- or double-matted and trimmed with decorative-edged scissors.

BASIC SUPPLIES: Adhesive; acrylic paints; assortment of solid and patterned papers; journaling pen or marker; photos; scissors; purchased scrapbook album with pages included; makeup wedge sponge; decorative stencils; photo cropping templates

ADDITIONAL SUPPLIES: Pastel chalk sticks; assortment of die-cuts; fine- and medium-point markers; flat paintbrush; ruler; decorative-edged scissors; alphabet stickers

"A BABE IN A HOUSE
IS A WELL-SPRING OF PLEASURE,
A MESSENGER OF PEACE AND LOVE,
A RESTING PLACE
FOR INNOCENCE ON EARTH,
A LINK BETWEEN ANGELS AND MEN."
— M. F. TUPPER

"YOU MADE MY WHOLE BEING;
YOU FORMED ME IN MY MOTHER'S BODY;
I PRAISE YOU BECAUSE YOU MADE ME
IN AN AMAZING AND WONDERFUL WAY."
— PSALM 139:13-14

1 Using decorative stencils and acrylic paints, stencil a double bow, a teddy bear, a rattle, a pacifier, and seven small stars onto white card stock.

2 Cut out the stenciled motifs and mat as desired.

3 Using a pastel chalk stick and a flat paint-brush, accent the teddy bear's cheeks.

4 Using an appropriate adhesive, adhere the photos to the backs of the photo frames, po-sitioning the photos in the windows as desired. Mat the framed photos. Combinations of coordi-nating and contrasting colors add interest. Use an assortment of decorative-edged scissors to trim the mats.

5 Arrange the page as desired and adhere the framed photos and stenciled motifs in place on a background page preprinted with tiny stars.

6 Using a ruler, draw lines and bows from the double bow to the small stenciled stars so the stars appear to be hanging.

1 Using decorative stencils and acrylic paints, stencil two teddy bears and a baby block onto white card stock. Add eyes and a mouth on each teddy bear.

2 Cut out the stenciled motifs and mat as desired. Stencil the words "Name, Date, Time, Weight, and Length" onto paper that has a baby bottle preprinted onto it.

3 Cut out the baby bottle and mat. Cut out and mat a second "baby bottle" to use as a frame for a favorite photo. Use decorative-edged scissors to trim the mats.

4 Using various patterned and solid papers, cut out stars in various sizes.

5 Arrange the page as desired and adhere the photo frame and stenciled motifs in place on a solid background page.

6 Randomly stencil small stars around the motifs.

7 Using an appropriate adhesive, adhere the photo in place on the photo frame and add the birth statistics with a journaling pen or marker.

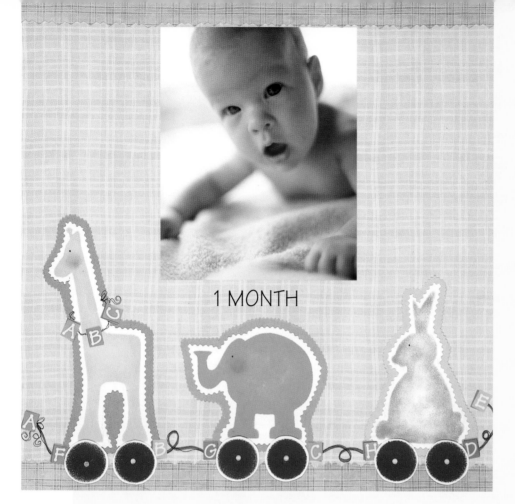

1 MONTH

1 Using decorative-edged scissors, trim 1" strips of patterned paper to fit across the top and bottom of the background page and adhere in place.

2 Using decorative stencils and acrylic paints, stencil a giraffe, an elephant, a bunny, and six circles (for wheels) onto white card stock.

3 Cut out the stenciled motifs and mat as desired. Punch a small hole in the center of each wheel.

4 Using a pastel chalk stick and a flat paintbrush, accent the animals' cheeks. Using a fine-point black marker, add a dot to make the eyes.

5 Arrange the page as desired and adhere the stenciled motifs in place on a background page preprinted with wiggly lines.

6 As shown above, place alphabet stickers around the giraffe's neck and along the bottom to make a pull toy. Using a fine-point black marker, draw lines to connect the alphabet stickers around the giraffe's neck and add a bow. Draw a pull string between the animal "cars" and draw a bow in the front. Using a medium-point brown marker, trace over the pull string between the animal cars.

7 As desired, the photo(s) can be single- or double-matted and trimmed with decorative-edged scissors.

8 Using an appropriate adhesive, adhere the photo(s) in place.

1 Using decorative stencils and acrylic paints, stencil four bows onto white card stock to closely match the bows around the outside of the preprinted paper. Stencil white checks onto the stenciled bows.

2 Cut out the stenciled bows.

3 Using a pastel chalk stick and a flat paintbrush, accent the cheeks and inside the ears of a bunny die-cut. Using a fine-point black marker, color the bunny's nose.

4 Mat the bunny die-cut as desired.

5 Arrange the page as desired and adhere the stenciled bows and bunny die-cut in place on a background page preprinted with flowers and bows.

6 Using an appropriate adhesive, adhere the photo(s) in place.

7 If desired, the stenciled bows can be used as photo corners.

"BABIES
COME INTO THIS WORLD
HOLDING JOY IN THEIR HANDS.
AND WHEN
THEY OPEN
THOSE SMALL FINGERS,
THE WHOLE WORLD'S
SUPPLY IS
REPLENISHED
AGAIN."
— AUTHOR UNKNOWN

1 Using decorative stencils and acrylic paints, stencil three diaper pins, two ducks, and a segmented ribbon onto white card stock.

2 Cut out the stenciled motifs and mat as desired.

3 Using a pastel chalk stick and a flat paintbrush, accent the ducks' cheeks.

4 Arrange the page as desired and adhere the stenciled motifs in place on a background page preprinted with small checks.

5 As desired, the photo(s) can be single- or double-matted and trimmed with decorative-edged scissors.

6 Using an appropriate adhesive, adhere the photo(s) in place.

1 Using decorative-edged scissors, trim 1" strips of patterned paper to fit around the perimeter of the background page and adhere in place.

2 Using decorative stencils and acrylic paints, stencil a giraffe, an elephant, a bunny, and a teddy bear onto white card stock.

3 Cut out the stenciled motifs.

4 On a four-piece train die-cut, stencil small stars inside the wheels of the three cargo cars. As shown above, stencil three hearts on the engine. Stencil a heart on one cargo car door and one star on another cargo car door.

5 Mat the train die-cuts as desired and add the stenciled animals inside the train.

6 Arrange the page as desired and adhere the stenciled motifs in place on a background page preprinted with a pastel plaid.

7 As desired, the photo(s) can be single- or double-matted and trimmed with decorative-edged scissors.

8 Using an appropriate adhesive, adhere the photo(s) in place.

EMBELLISHING & BINDING THE COVER

1 Disassemble a purchased scrapbook album. Remove the spine.

2 Cut a piece of cotton fabric to cover the outside of the spine. Cut a piece of cotton fabric to the dimensions necessary to cover the front and the back of the album, allowing at least one inch on all sides for folding over to the inside of the album.

3 Place the cotton fabric, right side down, on a clean, flat surface that has been covered with waxed paper to protect it. Center the front of the album over the fabric. Bring the edges of the fabric around to the inside of the album cover. Using a hot-glue gun, adhere in place. To reduce bulk, clip and miter the corners. Repeat the process to cover the back of the album and the spine.

4 Adhere card stock that has been cut to fit the inside of the album cover to hide the raw edges of the fabric. If desired, the card stock can be covered with coordinating or contrasting cotton fabric.

5 Adhere rickrack trim down the front of the album cover as desired.

6 Using decorative stencils and acrylic paints, stencil a teddy bear, a diaper pin, a baby bib, and a pacifier onto white cotton fabric. Cut out leaving a $1/4$" border. Turn the edges under and adhere onto white felt. Using pinking shears, trim around the stenciled motifs leaving a $1/4$" border.

7 Adhere the stenciled motifs to the front of the album cover as desired, randomly placing satin ribbon behind the motifs. The ribbon should be free-flowing between the motifs and adhered into position. If desired, simple buttons can be adhered to the sides of the stenciled baby bib.

8 Place the completed scrapbook pages in the desired order and place them inside the album cover. Reassemble the purchased scrapbook album, replacing the fabric-covered spine.

Photo shown on page 38.

SUPPLIES FOR EMBELLISHING THE COVER: Card stock; decorative stencils; cotton fabric; felt; hot-glue gun and glue sticks; makeup wedge sponge; acrylic paints; pinking shears; rickrack trim; scissors; purchased scrapbook album with pages included; waxed paper

"CHILDREN ARE MEANT TO BE SEEN, HEARD, AND BELIEVED."
— AUTHOR UNKNOWN

SHARE

SEWN

HOME

THREAD OF LIFE

"FRIENDSHIP IS THE THREAD IN THE PATCHWORK OF LIFE."
— AUTHOR UNKNOWN

STITCHING ON PAPER

1 Choose solid papers to be used as the background pages so all of the stitching lines will be visible. Using an appropriate adhesive, adhere the chosen background pages to the album pages.

2 First, stitch lines can be drawn with a fine-point marker. This allows many different styles of stitching to be done on the background page. In addition, any color combinations can be used.

3 Second, stitch lines can actually be sewn onto the background page with a sewing machine. This method is best suited for the experienced seamstress or tailor and great care must be taken so the card stock does not tear during the sewing process.

4 Images or motifs can be added to the background pages to enhance the stitching with acrylic paints or stencil creams. The use of cut-outs and die-cuts will add interest to the background page and can be matted to add dimension.

5 Using several mats behind the photos or the motifs will help render a "quilted" look. When choosing the patterned papers to be used as motifs, make certain to choose patterns that resemble fabric designs and patterns.

6 Once the photos have been cropped to the desired shapes and sizes, adhere them to the layered photo mats or photo frames. As desired, the photos can be trimmed with decorative-edged scissors.

BASIC SUPPLIES: Adhesive; assortment of solid and patterned card stock and papers; fine- and medium-point markers; pencil; journaling pen or marker; photos; scissors; photo cropping templates

ADDITIONAL SUPPLIES: Stencil creams; assortment of cut-outs or die-cuts; makeup wedge sponge; memorabilia; flat paintbrushes; acrylic paints; ruler; decorative-edged scissors; sewing machine; assortment of threads

...holy night...

...silent night...

...all is calm...

...all is bright...

ANGEL & SNOWMAN
Shown on pages 48 and 49.

1 Use two sheets of forest green card stock for the background pages. Cut 1/2" off each side of two sheets of red paper with wiggly white lines forming checks. Cut 1/2" off one long side and 1/2" off one short side of one sheet of navy blue card stock and one sheet of navy blue paper with white stars. Beginning with the forest green card stock, layer the trimmed sheets. One sheet of the red paper with checks goes on each background page. Only one sheet of each of the navy blue papers goes on each background paper. Using an appropriate adhesive, adhere all pages in position as shown.

2 Make a photo mat by layering red paper with checks, navy blue card stock, and red paper with red stars. Cut each mat with different borders ranging from 1/8" to 1". Adhere the photo to the center of the photo mat.

3 Make a photo mat by layering forest green handmade paper with fibers, navy blue card stock, and white paper with red stripes. Cut each mat with different borders ranging from 1/8" to 1/2". Adhere the photo to the center of the photo mat.

4 As shown on pages 48 and 49, adhere the photo mats at an angle on the background pages. Trim around the outside edges of the background page if excess paper and card stock extends off the page.

5 Trace the Snowman, Small Star, Small Heart, and Moon Patterns from page 51 and shown at right onto aged parchment card stock and cut out. You need one snowman, five small stars, two small hearts, and one moon. Trace the Angel's Face, Wings, Hands, and Feet Patterns onto aged parchment card stock and cut out. Trace the Small Tree and the Large Tree Patterns onto forest green handmade paper and cut out. Trace the Snowman's Scarf and the Angel's Heart Patterns onto white paper with red stripes and cut out. Trace the Snowman's Heart and the Angel's Body and Sleeve Patterns onto red-and-black plaid paper and cut out. Trace the Angel's Petticoat Pattern onto red paper with red stars and cut out. Trace the Large Star Pattern onto red paper with white stars and cut out. Mat the large star with aged parchment card stock and trim to a 1/4" border.

6 As shown, adhere the motifs on the background pages, overlapping as desired.

7 Using a fine-point black marker, draw the snowman's and angel's faces according to the patterns. Add stitch lines around the snowman, angel, stars, tree tops, and moon. Using a medium-point gold marker, write the words and draw the angel's hair. Add dots around the corners of the border as desired.

8 Using acrylic paints, add highlights and detail to the snowman's and angel's faces and around the motifs as desired.

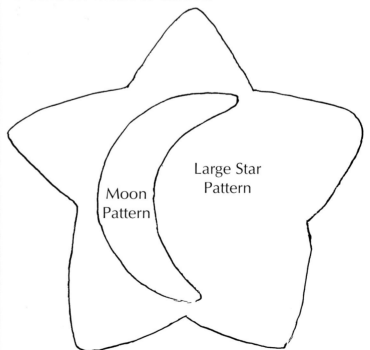

Moon Pattern

Large Star Pattern

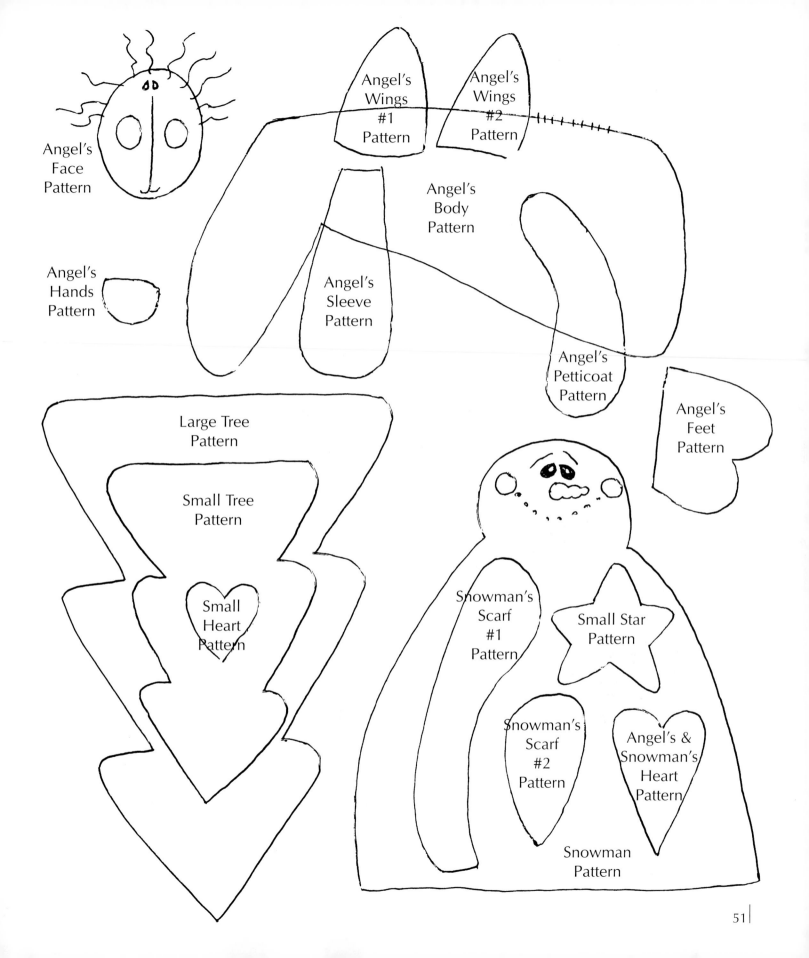

Angel's Face Pattern

Angel's Wings #1 Pattern

Angel's Wings #2 Pattern

Angel's Body Pattern

Angel's Hands Pattern

Angel's Sleeve Pattern

Angel's Petticoat Pattern

Angel's Feet Pattern

Large Tree Pattern

Small Tree Pattern

Small Heart Pattern

Snowman's Scarf #1 Pattern

Small Star Pattern

Snowman's Scarf #2 Pattern

Angel's & Snowman's Heart Pattern

Snowman Pattern

happy holidays and new year ....

1 Use a sheet of green parchment card stock for the background page.

2 Make a photo mat by layering dark red paper with black lines and dots, forest green card stock with wiggly lines, and red card stock with wiggly lines. Cut each mat with different borders ranging from $^1/_8$" to $^1/_2$". Using an appropriate adhesive, adhere the photo to the center of the photo mat.

3 Make a photo mat by layering red card stock with wiggly lines and forest green card stock with poinsettias. Cut each mat with different borders ranging from $^1/_4$" to $^1/_2$". Adhere the photo to the center of the photo mat. As shown on page 52, use different shapes for the photos and photo mats or frames to add interest to each page.

4 As shown above, adhere the photo mats on the background page.

5 Trace one Holly Leaf Pattern shown below onto forest green card stock with black lines and one onto forest green card stock with wiggly lines and cut out. Trace the Holly Berry Pattern onto red card stock with wiggly lines and cut out. You need three berries. Trace the Cardinal and Car-dinal's Wing Patterns onto dark red card stock with black lines and cut out. Trace the Cardinal's Beak Pattern onto dark orange card stock and cut out. Trace the Button Pattern onto any scrap of light colored card stock and cut out. Adhere the cardinal's beak in place. Mat the cardinal and the cardinal's wing with black card stock and trim to a $^1/_8$" border.

6 As shown, adhere the motifs on the background page, overlapping as desired.

7 Using a fine-point green marker, draw the details on the button and draw the cardinal's eye. Add stitch lines around one of the photo mats. Write the words to border the other photo mat. Using a fine-point white marker, draw accent lines on the cardinal, cardinal's beak and wing, and the holly leaves and berries.

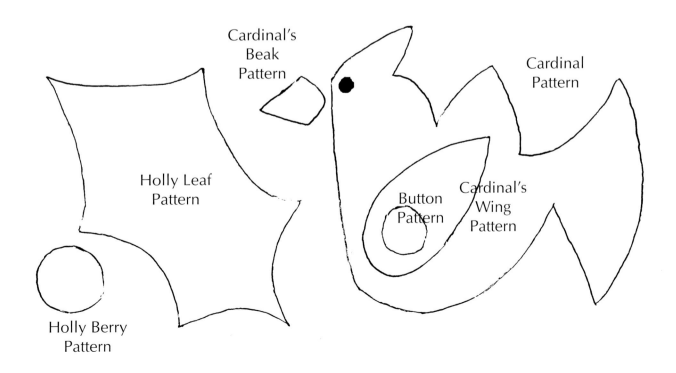

Cardinal's
Beak
Pattern

Cardinal
Pattern

Holly Leaf
Pattern

Button
Pattern

Cardinal's
Wing
Pattern

Holly Berry
Pattern

1 Use a sheet of parchment card stock for the background page.

2 Cut a pocket to the desired size from a sheet of vellum. Using a sewing machine, sew the pocket to the background page with a basting stitch. Choose a sewing thread color that coordinates or contrasts with the background page.

3 Using an appropriate adhesive, adhere a bow and ribbon die-cut that has been cut from a patterned paper across the top of the background page.

4 Using a fine-point black marker, add stitch lines around the bow and ribbon die-cut.

5 Use the pocket to store precious memorabilia such as newspaper clippings, birth announcements, etc.

1 Use a sheet of parchment card stock for the background page.

2 Using a ruler and a pencil, divide the page into sections that will accommodate the photos you are using. Using a sewing machine, sew the lines on the background page with a basting stitch. Choose a sewing thread color that coordinates or contrasts with the background page.

3 Using acrylic paints, randomly wash several of the "boxes" with coordinating and contrasting colors.

4 Using an appropriate adhesive, randomly adhere the photos to the background page.

EMBELLISHING & BINDING THE COVER

1. The front and back covers for this scrapbook album are made from card stock.

2. Using an appropriate adhesive, single- or double-mat a photo and trim with decorative-edged scissors. Adhere the photo mat to the card stock that has been chosen for the front cover of the scrapbook album.

3. Using a large-eyed needle and three to six strands of embroidery floss to coordinate with the photo mats, add decorative stitching as desired. It should appear that the stitching actually holds the photo mat to the album cover.

4. Add buttons or other charms to the album cover as desired.

5. Place the completed scrapbook pages in the desired order and place them between the front and the back album covers. Using embroidery floss that coordinates with the photo mats, bind the album together by stitching through all of the pages.

Photo shown on page 46.

SUPPLIES FOR EMBELLISHING THE COVER: Adhesive; assortment of buttons; assortment of card stock; embroidery floss; large-eyed needle; photos; scissors; decorative-edged scissors; photo cropping templates

"BUTTONS AND PATCHES
AND THE COLD WIND BLOWING
THE DAYS PASS QUICKLY
WHEN I AM SEWING."
— AUTHOR UNKNOWN

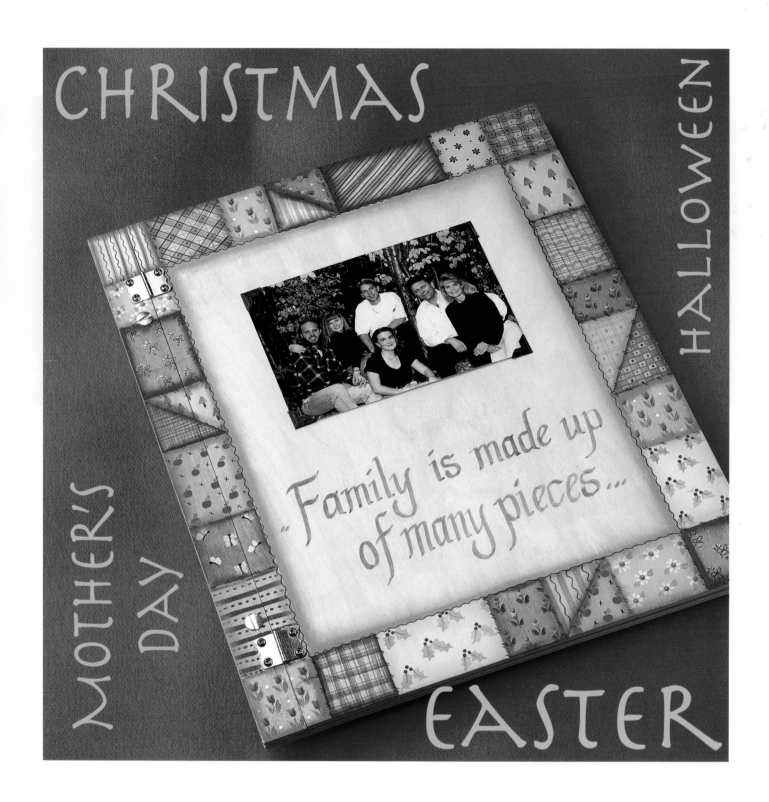

CHRISTMAS

HALLOWEEN

Family is made up of many pieces...

MOTHER'S DAY

EASTER

"IN EVERY SEASON OF LIFE,
THERE IS SOMETHING TO CELEBRATE."
— AUTHOR UNKNOWN

TOLE PAINTING

Using the patterns provided, enlarge and transfer all necessary designs onto the album pages, using transfer paper and the small end of a stylus. Using a fine-point black marker, ink (outline) the designs. If desired, experienced tole painters can use a scroller or liner brush and paint that has been thinned to an inky consistency to do all of the linework.

Paint the designs according to the Tole Painting Terms on page 69 and the colors called for in the individual project directions. Seal-

ing the painted surface is not necessary and is not recommended because it tends to discolor the album pages.

Once the photos have been cropped to the desired shapes and sizes, adhere them directly to the background pages or to card stock for matting. As desired, the photos can be single- or double-matted and trimmed with decorative-edged scissors.

BASIC SUPPLIES: Adhesive; assortment of card stock; pastel chalk sticks; fine-point black markers; assortment of flat paintbrushes; acrylic paints; journaling pen or marker; photos; scissors; decorative-edged scissors; purchased scrapbook album with pages included; scroller or liner brush; stylus; photo cropping templates; old toothbrush; transfer paper

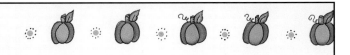

1 Copy the Pumpkin Border Pattern from page 66 and transfer the designs onto the background page. Using a fine-point black marker, ink the designs.

2 Using acrylic paints, wash the pumpkins with orange, the stems with straw, and the leaves with green. Shade the pumpkins with red orange, the stems with golden brown, and the leaves with green.

3 Using the handle of the paintbrush or a stylus, make dots between the pumpkins with golden brown.

4 Using the fine-point black marker, add tiny accent dots around each large dot.

5 As desired, the photos can be single- or double-matted and trimmed with decorative-edged scissors. Using an appropriate adhesive, adhere the photos in place.

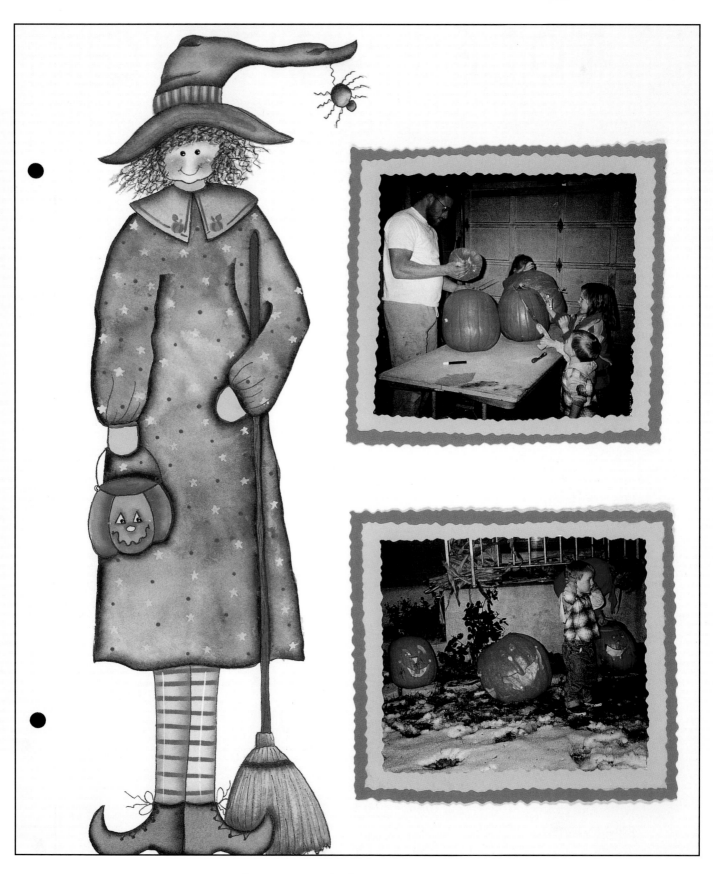

Halloween Witch directions on page 60.

Fall Harvest Scarecrow directions on pages 60-61.

HALLOWEEN WITCH
Shown on page 58.

1 Enlarge the Witch Pattern from page 67 and transfer the design onto the background page. Using a fine-point black marker, ink the design.

2 Using acrylic paints, wash the witch's hair, shoes, and the spider with black, the witch's socks and the jack-o-lantern's eyes and nose with yellow, the straw on the broom with honey brown, the broom handle with brown, the weaving string on the broom with red, the witch's hat band and the jack-o-lantern with orange, the witch's face, neck, and hands with flesh, and the witch's dress, collar, and hat with purple. Shade the witch's hair, shoes, dress, collar, hat, and the spider with black, the witch's socks with honey brown, the broom with burnt sienna, the jack-o-lantern and the witch's hat band with red orange, and the witch's face, neck, and hands with dark flesh.

3 Add horizontal stripes on the witch's socks with red orange; add one vertical highlight stripe on each sock with white. Add vertical stripes on the witch's hat band with purple and yellow. Stroke streaks on the broom with yellow.

4 Using a stylus, add dots for the witch's eyes with black and randomly add tiny dots on the witch's dress with red orange. Randomly add small stars between each tiny dot with yellow.

5 Paint one small pumpkin on each side of the witch's collar with orange, then shade them with red orange. Paint the stems and the leaves with green. Add stripes on the witch's collar with purple.

6 Using a pastel chalk stick and a flat paint-brush, accent the witch's cheeks and highlight the witch's eyes with a little dot of white.

7 As desired, the photos can be single- or double-matted and trimmed with decorative-edged scissors. Using an appropriate adhesive, adhere the photos in place.

FALL HARVEST SCARECROW
Shown on page 59.

1 Enlarge the Scarecrow Pattern from page 66 and transfer the design onto the background page. Using a fine-point black marker, ink the design. Write the words on the sign.

2 Using acrylic paints, wash the scarecrow's face, gloves, shirt, and the sign with beige, the scarecrow's hair and boots with golden brown, the birds with black plus white, the scarecrow's hat, the sunflower petals, and the birds' beaks with straw, the scarecrow's overalls with dark blue, the scarecrow's nose and scarf with orange, the sunflower stem and leaves with green, and the center of the sunflower with burnt sienna. Shade the scarecrow's face with brown plus beige, the scarecrow's hair, hat, boots, gloves, the sign, the center of the sunflower, and the birds' beaks with burnt sienna, the scarecrow's shirt with brown, the scarecrow's scarf with orange, the birds with black plus a little white, the bottom of the scarecrow's nose with orange plus red, the scarecrow's pants with dark blue, and the sunflower leaves with green.

3 Add stripes on the scarecrow's shirt alternately with a wash of blue and a wash of orange. Using a scroller and paint that has been thinned to an inky consistency, add thin stripes of the same colors through the center of each washed stripe. Add a thin brown stripe between each washed stripe. Add horizontal and verticals stripes on the scarecrow's scarf with orange plus a little red.

4 Using the scroller, add wood grain to the sign with brown, lines on the sunflower petals and texture on the scarecrow's hat with golden

brown. Pull straw from the scarecrow's sleeves with golden brown, straw, and white. Pull lines for the bird's nest with straw.

5 Dry-brush the scarecrow's overalls and boots with off-white. Using a stylus, add dots for the scarecrow's and birds' eyes with black. Make tiny dots around the center of the sunflower with black.

6 Using a pastel chalk stick and a flat paint-brush, accent the scarecrow's cheeks.

7 Using an old toothbrush, spatter the entire background page with brown and orange. Mask the scarecrow to prevent splatters.

8 As desired, the photo(s) can be single- or double-matted and trimmed with decorative-edged scissors. Using an appropriate adhesive, adhere the photo(s) in place.

EASTER BUNNY
Shown on page 62.

1 Enlarge the Easter Bunny and Rosebud Pattern from page 68 and the transfer designs onto the background page (randomly placing the rose-buds). Using a fine-point black marker, ink the designs.

2 Using acrylic paints, wash each rosebud with pink and the leaves with green. Wash the bunny with antique white, the bunny's shirt with white, the bunny's handkerchief, the small stripes on the Easter egg, and the leaves on the rose-buds (on the Easter egg) with green, the bunny's overalls, the blue stripe on the Easter egg, and the paint in the middle paint bucket with blue, the stripe at the top of the Easter egg and the paint on the end of the paintbrush with teal, two stripes on the Easter egg and the paint in the first paint bucket with lavender, the bunny's nose and the stripe on the Easter egg with rosebuds with

pink, the paintbrush bristles with golden brown, the ferrule of the paintbrush and the paint buck-ets with gray, the brush handle with red, the rose-buds on the pink stripe on the Easter egg with dark pink, and the last stripe on the Easter egg and the paint in the third paint bucket with yel-low. Shade the bunny with tan, the bunny's shirt, overalls, the blue stripe on the Easter egg, and the blue paint in the paint bucket with blue, the bunny's handkerchief, the two small stripes on the Easter egg, and the leaves on the rosebuds with green, the teal stripe on the Easter egg and the paint on the paintbrush with teal, the two lavender stripes on the Easter egg and the laven-der paint in the paint bucket with lavender, the pink stripe on the Easter egg with dark pink, and the yellow stripe on the Easter egg and the yel-low paint in the paint bucket with golden brown.

3 Shade the bunny's body, ears, handker-chief, the Easter egg, and the paint buckets with off-white.

4 Add stripes on the bunny's shirt by alternat-ing lavender, yellow, blue, and green.

5 Using a stylus, add dots for the bunny's eyes with black and accent dots between the rose-buds on the background page with yellow. Ran-domly add tiny dots on the handkerchief and, if desired, on one or two sections of the Easter egg with white. Paint the remaining sections of the Easter egg with squiggles, stripes, or flowers, as desired.

6 Using a pastel chalk stick and a flat paint-brush, accent the bunny's cheeks and inside the bunny's ears and highlight the bunny's eyes with a little dot of off-white.

7 As desired, the photos can be single- or double-matted and trimmed with decorative-edged scissors. Using an appropriate adhesive, adhere the photos in place.

Easter Bunny directions on page 61.

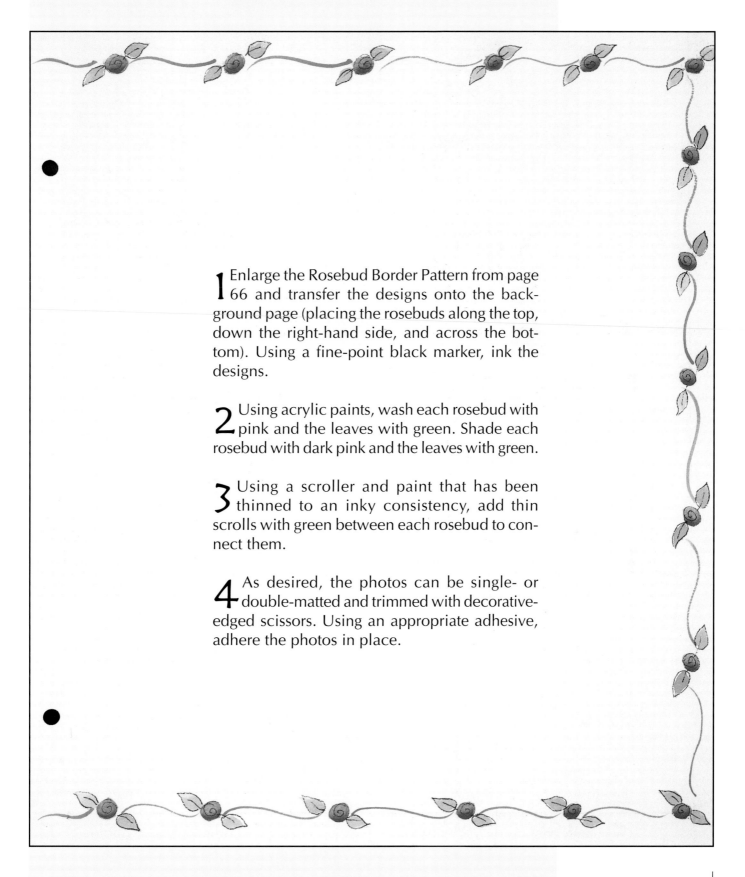

1 Enlarge the Rosebud Border Pattern from page 66 and transfer the designs onto the background page (placing the rosebuds along the top, down the right-hand side, and across the bottom). Using a fine-point black marker, ink the designs.

2 Using acrylic paints, wash each rosebud with pink and the leaves with green. Shade each rosebud with dark pink and the leaves with green.

3 Using a scroller and paint that has been thinned to an inky consistency, add thin scrolls with green between each rosebud to connect them.

4 As desired, the photos can be single- or double-matted and trimmed with decorative-edged scissors. Using an appropriate adhesive, adhere the photos in place.

"WRAP YOURSELF IN THE WARMTH OF THE SEASON."
—AUTHOR UNKNOWN

1 Using acrylic paints, base-paint the background page with bright red. Wash large horizontal and vertical stripes evenly spaced with dark green.

2 Add thin horizontal and vertical stripes with bright green and dark yellow to create a Tartan plaid.

3 Reduce the Holly Leaf Pattern from page 53 and then transfer the designs onto white card stock. Make two holly designs for each photo to be used.

4 Wash, then shade, each holly leaf with bright green. Wash, then shade, each holly berry with bright red.

5 Using a stylus, add one tiny accent dot with metallic gold on each holly berry.

6 Using an appropriate adhesive, adhere the photos in place and add the holly photo corners in opposite corners of each photo.

1 Enlarge the Package Bow Patterns from page 67 and transfer the designs onto the background page. Using a fine-point black marker, ink the designs.

2 Using acrylic paints, wash, then highlight, each bow. Wash, then highlight, one bow with green and shade with dark green, wash, then highlight, one bow with blue and shade with dark blue, and wash, then highlight, one bow with red and shade with burgundy. Wash the gift tag with off-white, then shade it with light brown.

3 Using paint thinned to an inky consistency, add the thread that leads to the gift tag with red. Using the same marker, add stitch lines around the gift tag and write "To:" and "From:" on the gift tag.

4 As shown above, round the top two corners on the photo (package) with the green bow. Leave the photos unmatted so they look like presents.

5 Using an appropriate adhesive, adhere the photos in place.

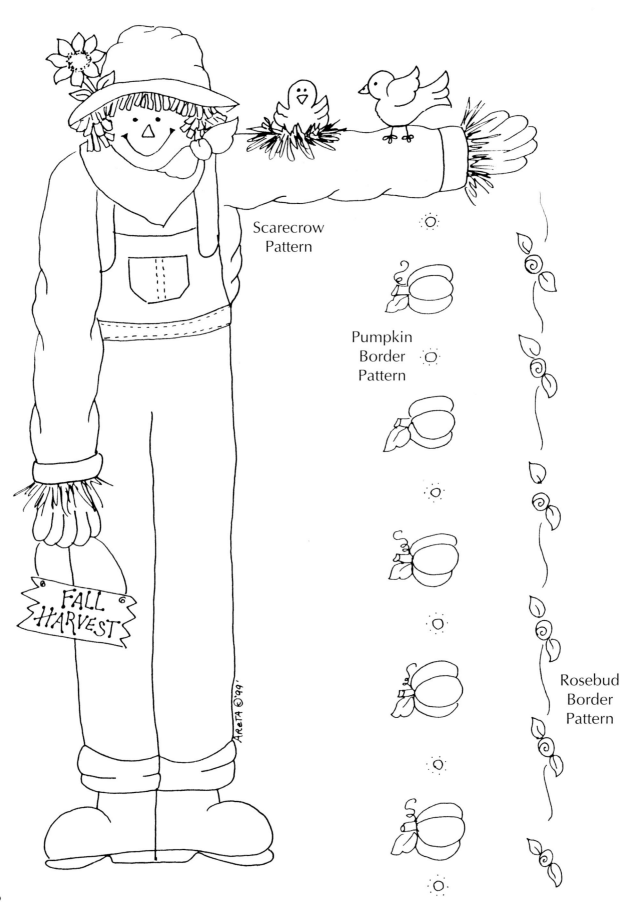

Scarecrow
Pattern

Pumpkin
Border
Pattern

Rosebud
Border
Pattern

FALL
HARVEST

AReTA ©'99'

66

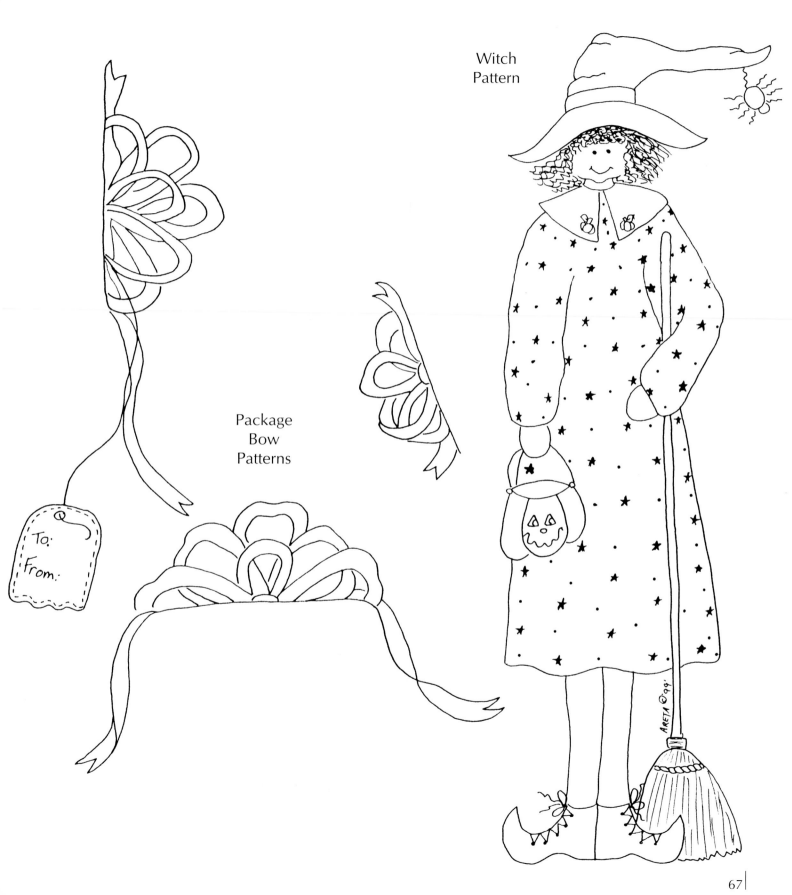

Package
Bow
Patterns

Witch
Pattern

Easter Bunny
and Rosebud
Pattern

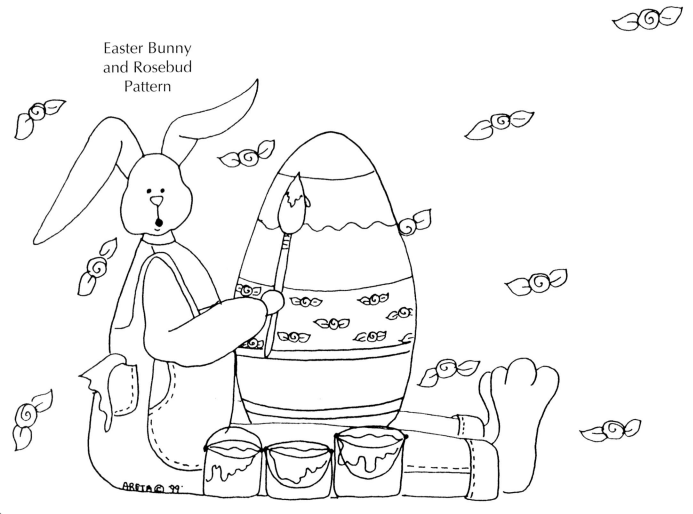

ARETA © 99

TOLE PAINTING TERMS

BASE PAINT: Paint over any area with paint as many times as necessary until opaque coverage is achieved.

DOT: Using the end of a paintbrush, a stylus, or a toothpick, dip in paint. Touch any area to make a dot. The handle of a paintbrush will produce large dots and a toothpick will produce very small dots.

DRY BRUSH: Load an old fluffy flatbrush with paint. Stroke the flatbrush over a paper towel to remove excess paint. Brush over any area in a slip-slap motion.

FLOAT: Using the largest flatbrush appropriate for the area being painted (never smaller than a #6), load it with water. On a paper towel that has been folded in fourths, blot excess water until the shine from the water is absorbed. Load one side of the flatbrush with paint. Stroke the brush toward you on the palette to soften the color. One side should have strong color and the other side should be clear water.

HIGHLIGHT: Using a lighter shade of the same color as the "wash," float over specific areas to highlight the image.

INK: Using a fine-point permanent marker, outline the transferred pattern designs. Experienced tole painters can use a scroller or liner brush and paint that has been thinned to an inky (watercolor) consistency to do all of the linework.

SHADE: Using the same color as (or slightly darker than) the "wash," float a shade over specific areas to enhance the image. If the wash is too dark, use a darker shade of the same color.

SPATTER: Using an old toothbrush and paint that has been thinned with water to an inky (watercolor) consistency, load the toothbrush and blot on a paper towel to absorb excess paint. Stroke over the bristles of the toothbrush with your finger to "spatter" over any dry, painted surface.

WASH: Paint over any area with paint that has been thinned with water to an inky (watercolor) consistency. Painting should be done quickly and should not be overworked or the paint has a tendency to lift and create "holes" in the color.

EMBELLISHING & BINDING THE COVER

1 Remove the album pages from a purchased scrapbook album made from wood. Using acrylic paints and various sized flat paintbrushes, paint the border around the outside of the scrapbook album.

2 Beginning in the upper left-hand corner, wash, then shade, the first square with off-white. Add thick stripes, then thin stripes with orange. Add wavy stripes with black.

3 Wash, then shade, the second square with green. Add large diagonal stripes, then thin horizontal and vertical stripes with green. Add thin diagonal stripes and tiny dots with red.

4 Wash, then shade, the third square with light pink. Paint the tulips with medium pink and the stems and leaves with green. Shade the tulips with dark pink and add small dots with white.

Wash half of the fourth square (at a diagonal) with light ivory, then shade it with red. Add large stripes with a wash of red and thin stripes with green. Wash, then shade, the remaining half of the diagonal with medium purple. Add the flower "dots" with light purple and the leaves with green. Outline the flowers with medium purple and add small dots with white.

The next "square" will become a "rectangle" because it should take up the space of two squares. Wash, then shade, the fifth square with red. Add large diagonal stripes with white and thin stripes alternately with red and green.

Wash the sixth square with straw then shade it with golden brown. Add large dots with orange and very small dots with black.

The seventh square is the last square across the top of the scrapbook album. Wash, then shade, with orange. Add horizontal and vertical stripes with a darker wash of orange. Add wavy stripes and tiny dots with black. Add tiny dots with orange between the black dots.

Going down the right-hand side of the scrapbook album, wash, then shade, the eighth square with green. Paint triangles with green for trees and add the tree trunks with brown.

Wash the ninth square with tan, then shade it with brown. Add wavy stripes with a wash of brown and horizontal and vertical stripes alternately with orange and blue.

Wash, then shade, the tenth square with medium purple. Paint the rosebuds with light purple and the stems and leaves with green. Shade the rosebuds with medium purple.

Wash, then shade, half of the eleventh square (at a diagonal) with yellow green. Add horizontal and vertical stripes and small dots with yellow green. Wash, then shade, the remaining half of the diagonal with brown. Add horizontal and vertical stripes and small dots with brown. Wash every other square with brown to create checks.

Paint the twelvth square as with the third square.

Wash the thirteenth square with off-white, then shade it with golden brown. Paint the holly leaves with green and add accent veins. Add large dots with red for holly berries.

Wash, then shade, the fourteenth square with red. Paint the candy canes with off-white and stripes on the candy canes alternately with red and green. Add a bow to each candy cane with black.

Going right to left across the bottom of the scrapbook album, wash the fifteenth square with straw, then shade it with golden brown. Paint the daisies with off-white and add large dots with golden brown for the centers of the daisies. Add the leaves with green and add one tiny dot in each "center" to highlight.

Wash, then shade, half of the sixteenth square (at a diagonal) with green. Add large vertical stripes with green and thin wavy stripes with red. Wash, then shade, the remaining half of the diagonal with orange. Paint the pumpkins with red orange and the stems and leaves with green. Add small "x's" in between the pumpkins with black.

Paint the seventeenth square as with the tenth square.

Paint the eighteenth square as with the thirteenth square.

Wash the nineteenth square with tan, then shade it with brown. Add large horizontal and vertical stripes with brown. Add thin horizontal and vertical stripes alternately with orange and blue.

Paint the twentieth square as with the third square.

Going from bottom to top up the left-hand side of the scrapbook album, wash, then shade, the twenty-first square with yellow green. Add large horizontal stripes with red and dashes with green.

Wash, then shade, the twenty-second square with medium purple. Paint butterfly wings with off-white and add the heads and bodies with black.

Paint the twenty-third square as with the half of the sixteenth square that matches it.

Wash half of the twenty-fourth square (at a diagonal) with tan, then shade it with brown. Add several thin horizontal and vertical stripes with brown. Paint the remaining half of the diagonal as with the eighth square.

Paint the twenty-fifth square as with the fourteenth square.

Paint the twenty-sixth square as with the fifteenth square.

Wash the center section of the scrapbook album with off-white, then shade it with tan. Add a thin wavy border on the inside around the center section with black, then randomly add tiny stitches with black to make all of the "squares" look quilted.

As shown, adhere a photo to the front of the purchased scrapbook album and paint a favorite phrase below it. Insert the album pages back inside the scrapbook album.

Photo shown on page 56.

SUPPLIES FOR EMBELLISHING THE COVER: Liner brushes;
acrylic paints; flat and small round paintbrushes; purchased scrapbook album (made from wood) with pages included; scroller; stylus

SHARING

GOOD TIMES

FUN

TOGETHER

"BEAUTIFUL YOUNG PEOPLE ARE ACTS OF NATURE;
BEAUTIFUL OLD PEOPLE ARE WORKS OF ART."

— AUTHOR UNKNOWN

USING COLLAGE

1. The actual scrapbook album shown in this section is not one that has been purchased. The pages for this album were made from handmade (or rice) paper folded in an accordion style. The number of pages is optional.

2. Embellish each page in the scrapbook album with a variety of collage techniques. If the album has a theme, make certain to carry that theme throughout. This is easily achieved by using coordinating or contrasting color combinations and alternating them from page to page.

3. When using handmade or rice paper, and torn edges are desired, use water to wet the paper. This will aid in neatly tearing the handmade or rice paper. Depending on the durability of the paper being used, it may be necessary to reinforce the folded areas.

4. Once the photos have been cropped to the desired shapes and sizes, adhere them directly to the background pages or to card stock for matting. As desired, the photos can be single- or double-matted and trimmed with decorative-edged scissors.

BASIC SUPPLIES: Adhesive; soft filbert brush; stencil brush; stencil creams; glitter; gold leafing; mica flakes; large-eyed needle; flat paintbrushes; acrylic paints; rice paper; assortment of wrapping papers; journaling pen or marker; gold photo corners; photos; iridescent powders; silk ribbon; rivets and rivet gun; scissors; decorative-edged scissors; double-sided tape; photo cropping templates; metallic gold thread

"YOU'VE GOT TO SING LIKE NOBODY'S LISTENING
YOU'VE GOT TO LOVE LIKE YOU'LL NEVER GET HURT
YOU'VE GOT TO DANCE LIKE NOBODY'S WATCHING
YOU'VE GOT TO LIVE LIKE IT'S HEAVEN ON EARTH."
— AUTHOR UNKNOWN

1 Using a deckle-edged blade and a rotary cutter, cut several 1/4"- to 1/2"-wide strips from white rice paper. Tear one 2"-wide strip from white rice paper. Tear several pieces from a variety of decorative wrapping papers.

2 Using an appropriate adhesive, adhere the torn strips of white rice paper down the center (in the fold) of the double-page spread. Randomly adhere the pieces of wrapping paper to the background page.

3 Arrange the narrow strips of white rice paper diagonally across the background page. Using rivets and a rivet gun, attach each of the strips of rice paper at the edge of the background page. Repeat in the opposite diagonal direction so strips of rice paper form diamond-shaped openings.

4 Using a soft filbert brush, apply iridescent powders in some of the diamond-shaped openings. Affix the powder by spraying it with a light mist of water.

5 Using an appropriate adhesive, arrange the photos as desired and adhere in place.

"FOR MEMORY HAS PAINTED
THIS PERFECT DAY
WITH COLORS THAT NEVER FADE.
AND WE FIND AT THE END
OF A PERFECT DAY,
THE SOUL
OF A FRIEND WE'VE MADE."
— CARRIE JACOBS BOND

1 Tear several pieces from a variety of decorative wrapping papers and rice paper.

2 Using an appropriate adhesive, randomly adhere the pieces of wrapping paper and rice paper to the background page.

3 Crumple some pieces of gold leafing and adhere them in place on the background page as desired.

4 Randomly adhere mica flakes on the background page as desired.

5 Using stencil creams and a stencil brush, accent the background page with color.

6 Place double-sided tape over the background page as desired, then sprinkle it with glitter to completely cover the tape.

7 Using an appropriate adhesive and gold photo corners, arrange the photos as desired and adhere in place.

8 Attach a strand of metallic gold thread so it overlaps one or two of the photos. Make certain not to pull the strand of thread too tight, as a loose, free-flowing strand is desirable.

"FAMILY MEANS TOO MUCH,
FRIENDS ARE TOO VALUABLE,
AND LIFE IS TOO SHORT
TO PUT OFF SHARING WITH PEOPLE
HOW MUCH THEY REALLY MEAN TO YOU
AND PURSUING WHATEVER IT IS
THAT MAKES YOU HAPPY."

— AUTHOR UNKNOWN

1 Tear several 3"- to 4"-wide strips from off-white rice paper. Tear the tops of each strip unevenly so they look like the tops of mountains. Make certain each strip is long enough to fit the dimensions of the background page from side to side.

2 Using a soft filbert brush, apply iridescent powders to each of the "mountain-shaped" strips of rice paper. Affix the powder by spraying it with a light mist of water. Use a different color of iridescent powder for each section.

3 Using acrylic paints, paint the top edges of some of the rice paper sections with copper.

4 Using an appropriate adhesive, adhere the mountain-shaped strips of rice paper across the background page. Begin with the top strip and adhere only the bottom and side edges so the photos can be slipped behind each strip. Make certain to slightly overlap each strip.

5 Randomly adhere mica flakes on the background page as desired.

6 Place double-sided tape over the background page as desired, then sprinkle it with glitter to completely cover the tape.

7 Tear several pieces from a variety of decorative wrapping papers. Randomly adhere the pieces of wrapping paper to the background page. Using a large-eyed needle, sew a running-stitch with silk ribbon up the fold on the background page.

8 Using an appropriate adhesive, arrange the photos as shown and adhere in place.

9 Weave strands of metallic gold thread in and out of the silk ribbon stitches. Make certain not to pull the strands of thread too tight, as loose, free-flowing strands are desirable.

"WE HAVEN'T YET GOT EYES THAT CAN GAZE INTO ALL THE SPLENDOR THAT GOD HAS CREATED, BUT WE SHALL GET THEM ONE DAY, AND THAT WILL BE THE FINEST FAIRY TALE OF ALL, FOR WE SHALL BE IN IT OURSELVES."
— HANS CHRISTIAN ANDERSON

"EVERYONE IS AN ANGEL.
SIMPLY TAKE A MOMENT,
SPREAD YOUR WINGS, AND DISCOVER
HOW TRULY WONDERFUL LIFE CAN BE."
— AUTHOR UNKNOWN

1 Using a deckle-edged blade and a rotary cutter, cut several ¹/₄"- to ¹/₂"-wide strips from white rice paper.

2 Using a soft filbert brush, apply iridescent powders over the background page. Affix the powder by spraying it with a light mist of water.

3 Using copper acrylic paint, paint areas of the background page in a horizontal slip-slap motion.

4 Randomly adhere mica flakes on the background page as desired.

5 Place double-sided tape over the background page as desired, then sprinkle it with glitter to completely cover the tape.

6 Using an appropriate adhesive, arrange the photos as desired and adhere in place.

7 Arrange one narrow strip of white rice paper vertically down the right-hand side of the background page. Using rivets and a rivet gun, attach the strip of rice paper to the background page. Repeat with additional strips of rice paper, cut to the same length, to form photo corners.

8 Adhere a few strands of metallic gold thread and some silk ribbon to the background page. Make certain not to pull the strands of thread too tight, as loose, free-flowing strands are desirable.

1 Tear several pieces from a variety of decorative wrapping papers and handmade paper.

2 Using an appropriate adhesive, randomly adhere the pieces of wrapping paper and handmade paper to the background page. If desired, sew two pieces of the papers together with silk ribbon as shown above.

3 Crumple some pieces of gold leafing and adhere them in place on the background page as desired.

4 Using a stencil brush and stencil creams, accent the background page with color.

5 Using an appropriate adhesive and gold photo corners, arrange the photos as desired and adhere in place.

6 Adhere a strand of metallic gold thread so it overlaps one or two of the photos. Make certain not to pull the strand of thread too tight, as a loose, free-flowing strand is desirable.

EMBELLISHING & BINDING THE COVER

1 The binder and the pages for this scrapbook album become one piece once it has been assembled. Make certain to take every precaution to assure no errors are made while embellishing the album pages.

2 Using the cardboard core taken from an empty bolt of fabric, cut two pieces to the dimensions desired for the scrapbook album. Make certain each piece is the identical size as one piece will be used as the front cover and the other piece will be used as the back cover.

3 Using handmade or rice paper, cover the two pieces of cardboard as though you were wrapping a gift. Using an appropriate adhesive, seal each end. Using tape is not recommended.

4 Embellish the front cover as desired using techniques described in this section. If desired, a photo can also be added to the front cover of the scrapbook album.

5 To make the album pages, begin with a sheet of handmade or rice paper about three feet in length. Tear the paper across the top and the bottom to fit the dimensions of the scrapbook album from top to bottom. Using water to wet the edges will aid in neatly tearing the paper.

6 Once the paper is thoroughly dry, fold it in an accordion style. The number of pages is optional.

7 To assemble the scrapbook album, adhere the accordion-folded section to the inside of front cover and the inside of the back cover. This can be done before or after the individual album pages have been embellished. Tie with a decorative ribbon.

Photo shown on page 72.

SUPPLIES FOR EMBELLISHING THE COVER: Adhesive; cardboard; handmade or rice paper; ribbon; scissors; heavy-duty scissors

"HISTORY HAS PROVEN, GOD HAS NEVER GIVEN ANYONE A DREAM WITHOUT ALSO INCLUDING THE POWER TO ACHIEVE THAT DREAM; IT IS UP TO US TO CLAIM THE POWER AND GO AFTER THAT DREAM, OR JUST CLAIM IT WAS ONLY A DREAM."
— LARRY BENNETT

HERE KITTY KITTY
MEOW
PET'S
PURR
GONE FISHING

"EVERY LIFE SHOULD HAVE NINE CATS."
— AUTHOR UNKNOWN

USING COLORED PENCILS

1. Choose solid card stock to be used as the background pages.

2. Cut any freeform shapes desired from contrasting card stock. An alternative to cutting freeform objects is to use die-cuts or cut-outs.

3. Using colored pencils, embellish the background pages or accent all of the motifs (freeform objects, cut-outs, and die-cuts) that have been cut from contrasting card stock.

4. Once the photos have been cropped to the desired shapes and sizes, adhere them directly to the background pages.

BASIC SUPPLIES: Adhesive; assortment of bright colored card stock; journaling pen or marker; colored pencils (with a high wax content — similar to crayons); photos; scissors; purchased scrapbook album with pages included; photo cropping templates

ADDITIONAL SUPPLIES: Computer; craft knife; cutting mat; die-cuts or cut-outs; iron and ironing board; fine- and medium-point markers; paintbrushes; acrylic paints; white-out pen; decorative-edged scissors; towel

"A CHILD IS A PERSON
WHO CANNOT UNDERSTAND
WHY SOMEONE
WOULD GIVE AWAY
A PERFECTLY GOOD KITTEN."
— AUTHOR UNKNOWN

"EVERY DOG HAS HIS DAY, BUT THE NIGHTS ARE RESERVED FOR THE CATS."
—AUTHOR UNKNOWN

1 Using colored pencils, create a background pattern on one of the pages in the purchased scrapbook album. Draw lines on the background page with contrasting colors; the lines will have more character if you allow them to curve and bend. As shown above, if you have predetermined where the photo(s), artwork, etc., will be placed, those areas can be masked so the lines end at the masked-off areas.

2 Randomly add dots in the center of several of the "boxes" that were created by the intersection of the drawn lines.

3 On white paper or card stock, handwrite a phrase in an outlined fashion with a medium-point black marker or type the phrase on your computer, using a font that will allow it to be outlined. If using a computer, print out the phrase.

4 Using analogous colors, color in the outlined phrase, using heavy pressure. Cut out the colored images. Using a sharp craft knife, cut out the areas between the words.

5 Make a black and white photocopy of a favorite comic. Make it more interesting by coloring it as with any coloring book.

6 Arrange the page as desired and adhere the colored images in place on the background page.

7 Crop or silhouette the photos. As desired, the photos can be trimmed with decorative-edged scissors.

8 Using an appropriate adhesive, adhere the photos in place. Overlap the colored images and the photos as desired.

CATS ADD COLOR TO LIFE!

1 Make black-and-white photocopies of a favorite pet. Using colored pencils, add color to the black-and-white photocopies by lightly rubbing over the pictures with several colors.

2 On white paper or card stock, handwrite a phrase in an outlined fashion with a medium-point black marker or type the phrase on your computer, using a font that will allow it to be outlined. Choose one or two words and color in with the black marker to "fill in" the outline. If using a computer, choose one or two words that you will not outline, then print out the phrase.

3 Using analogous colors, color in the outlined and solid words, using heavy pressure. The colored pencil over the solid words will be muted in comparison to the colored pencil over the outlined words. Cut out and separate the colored images.

4 Crop or silhouette the photo(s) and black-and-white photocopies that have been colored. As desired, the photo(s) and/or photocopies can be trimmed with decorative-edged scissors.

5 Arrange the page as desired. Using an appropriate adhesive, adhere the photo(s) and/or photocopies in place on the background page.

6 Adhere the colored images in place. Overlap the colored images and the photos as desired.

7 Using colored pencils, create the "drop shadows" under and around the colored images with a cross-hatching technique.

1 Crop or silhouette the photos. As desired, the photos can be trimmed with decorative-edged scissors.

2 Arrange the page as desired. Using an appropriate adhesive, adhere the photos in place on the background page.

3 Using colored pencils, draw paw prints around one of the photos. Border the remaining photos with polka dots, swirls, dashes, lines,

etc. To enhance the images, outline them with a fine-point black marker.

4 Using colored pencils, write a phrase over and over across the top and bottom of the background page. To enhance the letters, trace over them with a fine-point black marker.

5 Using a white-out pen, add dots of white to add heavy contrast to the background page.

1 Cut a variety of freeform pets from card stock that contrasts with the background page. To cut a repeating row of pet shapes, fold the card stock into a fan shape as with paper dolls.

2 Using colored pencils, add details, such as tiger stripes, to the pets. Using a white-out pen, add eyes and teeth. Dot each eye with a fine-point black marker.

3 Crop or silhouette the photos. As desired, the photos can be trimmed with decorative-edged scissors.

4 Arrange the page as desired. Using an appropriate adhesive, adhere the photos and pets in place on the background page, overlapping as desired.

5 Using the white-out pen, write words on the pets and the background page.

"A CAT CAN PURR HIS WAY
OUT OF ANYTHING."
— AUTHOR UNKNOWN

1 Using acrylic paints and colored pencils, embellish the background page. Use the acrylic paints first, making certain not to apply them too thick. Let the acrylic paints dry thoroughly before using the colored pencils. If the acrylic paints should cause the background page to curl, place a towel on top of the page and iron it with medium-high heat.

2 Cut a photo frame from card stock in the shape of a wedge of cheese. Cut circles (windows) in the cheese to replicate Swiss cheese. Using an appropriate adhesive, adhere the photos to the back of the photo frame, positioning the photos in the windows as desired.

3 Cut a variety of freeform mice from card stock that contrasts with the background page.

4 Using colored pencils, add details to the mice. Dot the eyes and draw a mouth on each mouse with a fine-point black marker.

5 As shown above, cut the top from the wedge of cheese. Using colored pencils, write a phrase inside the top and bottom pieces of cheese. Add accent lines around the "holes" in the cheese.

6 Arrange the page as desired. Adhere the photo frame and mice in place on the background page, overlapping as desired.

"A MEOW
MASSAGES THE HEART."
— AUTHOR UNKNOWN

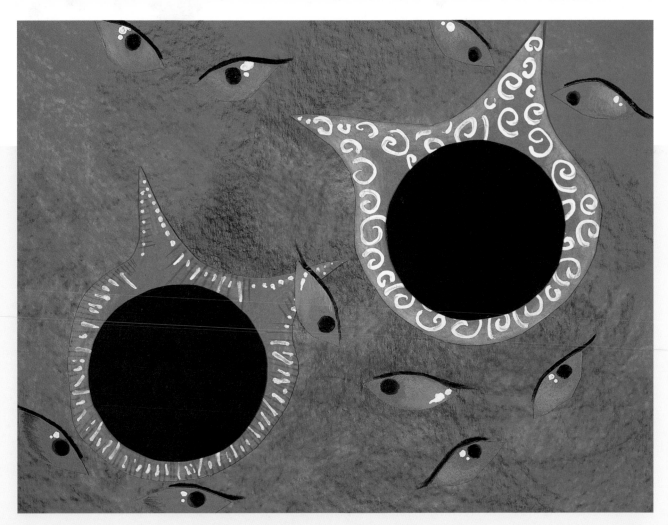

1 Using colored pencils, embellish the background page by rubbing or shading with the side of the pencil. Use at least four or five different colors. Use different surfaces underneath the background page to achieve various textures.

2 Cut two photo frames from card stock that contrasts with the background page in the shape of cat heads. Cut circles (windows) in the center of each photo frame. Using an appropriate adhesive, adhere the photos to the backs of the photo frames, positioning the photos in the windows as desired.

3 Using colored pencils, add cross-hatching and shading to the borders of the photo frames.

4 Using a white-out pen, add dots, lines, and swirls of white to add heavy contrast to the background page.

5 Cut several "cat eyes" from green card stock and color with colored pencils. Using a white-out pen, add dots in each eye. Draw each pupil with a fine-point black marker.

6 Arrange the page as desired. Adhere the photo frames and eyes in place on the background page, overlapping as desired. As shown above, add top eye liner with a medium-point black marker.

1 Using colored pencils, embellish the background page by drawing dashed lines in large
spirals to replicate balls of yarn. Use at least four
or five different colors.

2 Cut a freeform ball of yarn from card stock
that contrasts with the background page. Using colored pencils, draw lines on it to replicate
individual strands of yarn.

3 Arrange the page as desired. Using an appropriate adhesive, adhere the ball of yarn in
place on the background page, overlapping as
desired.

4 Crop or silhouette the photos. As desired,
the photos can be trimmed with decorative-
edged scissors.

5 Adhere the photos in place on the background page. As shown above, place one of
the photos on top of the ball of yarn.

EMBELLISHING & BINDING THE COVER

1 Cut a variety of freeform cats from card stock that coordinates with the background pages in the purchased scrapbook album. Cut a strip of freeform grass from green card stock. Cut a 3/4"-wide wavy strip from yellow card stock.

2 Using colored pencils, add details, such as tiger stripes, noses, eyebrows, and whiskers, to the cats. Dot each eye with a fine-point black marker. Add details to the strip of grass. Add dots and lines to the wavy strip.

3 Using an appropriate adhesive, adhere the cats and the wavy strip to the front of the purchased scrapbook album, overlapping as desired. The album shown has a square opening in the center of the front. Place a solid color of card stock on the inside to cover the opening and place one of the cats peering out from inside the album. Adhere the grass along the bottom of the album cover, tucking a few of the blades of grass underneath one of the cats as shown.

4 The album shown was purchased with a black cover which adds to the drama of this album when combined with the bright array of card stock colors that were used.

5 The album was purchased with a spiral binding, therefore the pages were created without removing them from the album. Make certain to take every precaution to assure no errors are made. In addition, the background pages inside the purchased scrapbook album were trimmed on the right-hand side in various geometric designs. This also adds to the drama of the album and adds intrigue and excitement — almost a whimsical look which is the perfect complement for any favorite pet album.

6 Attach an obsolete pet tag to the spiral binding.

Photo shown on page 84.

SUPPLIES FOR EMBELLISHING THE COVER:

Adhesive; assortment of bright colored card stock; fine-point black marker; colored pencils; scissors; purchased scrapbook album with pages included

"PEOPLE WHO HATE CATS
WILL COME BACK AS MICE
IN THEIR NEXT LIFE."
— AUTHOR UNKNOWN

"FOR WHEN THE GREAT SCORER COMES TO WRITE AGAINST YOUR NAME,
HE WRITES NOT THAT YOU WON OR LOST, BUT HOW YOU PLAYED THE GAME."
— GRANTLAND RICE

USING COMPUTER GRAPHICS

1 Choose solid papers to be used as the background pages. If the printer you are using can accommodate card stock weight, it is recommended for the background pages.

2 Begin by choosing a theme and then write down all the words you can think of to describe that subject. Using a computer, type the words. Use the same font for each word on the background page or, to be really daring, use different fonts for each word on the same page. The words can be upper and lower case, all caps, or all lower case.

3 Scan in all of the photos to be used or use the photos taken from a personal library of compact discs. Once the photos have been

4 cropped to the desired sizes, place them on the background page in your electronic file. If the use of a color printer is possible, the photos can be single- or double-matted as desired.

5 Begin placing the typed words around the placed photos. Some words should be placed at various angles.

6 When using the computer for page layouts and for journaling, color output is wonderful, but black-and-white output also creates tremendous results. Remember that when you use any output device, laser printers are recommended as the ink from ink jet printers will fade, smear, and smudge over time.

BASIC SUPPLIES: Computer; photos (scanned or on compact discs); printer — color or black-and-white; purchased scrapbook album with pages included

"SPORTS SHOULD ONLY BE PLAYED
ON DAYS THAT END WITH
THE LETTER Y."
— AUTHOR UNKNOWN

Baseball

strike out

GRAND SLAM

home run

Let's play golf

HOLE IN ONE

And you thought i couldn't be done!

CATCH & RELEASE

"FISHING IS MUCH MORE THAN FISH ...
IT IS THE GREAT OCCASION
WHEN WE MAY RETURN
TO THE FINE SIMPLICITY
OF OUR FOREFATHERS."
— HERBERT HOOVER

EMBELLISHING & BINDING THE COVER

1 Disassemble a purchased scrapbook album. The album was purchased with a spiral wire binding and the wire binding was removed.

2 Using a flat paintbrush and acrylic paint, paint the front and back covers of the album (inside and out) with two to three coats of black. Let the acrylic paint dry thoroughly between each coat.

3 Create the artwork for your album cover on the computer and print it out in black-and-white or in color, depending on the printer you are using. Trim to fit the album cover as desired.

4 Spray the artwork with a spray fixative to keep the ink from smearing. This is important whether you are using an ink jet printer or a laser printer. Let the spray fixative dry thoroughly.

5 Using a 1/2" flat paintbrush and découpage medium, découpage the artwork to the painted album cover. Apply the découpage medium to the back of the artwork, then carefully place it in position on the front of the album cover. Using a rubber brayer, remove the air pockets; then wipe off any excess découpage medium. Let the découpage medium dry thoroughly.

6 Apply another coat of découpage medium over the top of the artwork. Let the découpage medium dry thoroughly.

7 Place the completed scrapbook pages in the desired order and place them inside the album cover. Using ribbon that coordinates with the paint color of the album, lace the album together as with lacing shoes. Finish at the bottom with a simple knot.

Photo shown on page 94.

SUPPLIES FOR EMBELLISHING THE COVER: Rubber brayer; computer; découpage medium (matte finish); 1/2" flat paintbrush; acrylic paints; photos (scanned or on compact discs); printer — color or black-and-white; ribbon; scissors; purchased scrapbook album with pages included

"THE BEST AND MOST BEAUTIFUL THINGS IN THE WORLD
CANNOT BE SEEN OR EVEN TOUCHED.
THEY MUST BE FELT WITH THE HEART."
— HELEN KELLER

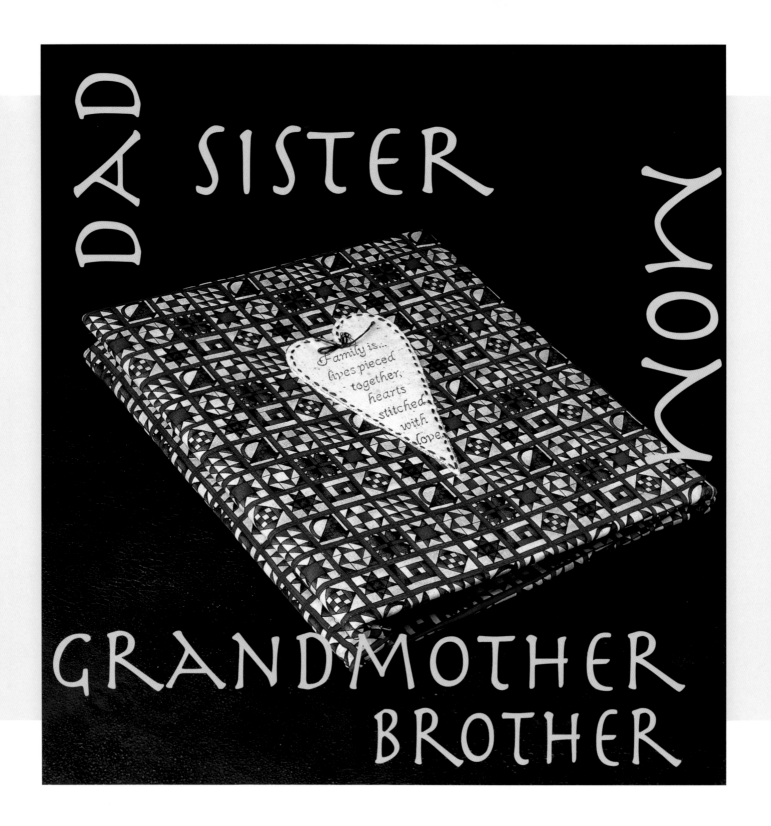

DAD SISTER MOM

Family is...
lives pieced
together,
hearts
stitched
with
love.

GRANDMOTHER
BROTHER

"HOME IS WHERE YOU HANG YOUR MEMORIES."
— AUTHOR UNKNOWN

USING FABRICS

1 Choose solid or patterned fabrics to be used as the background pages or as embellishments on the background pages.

2 Iron fusible web to the wrong side of the fabric. Cut out the fabric embellishments (motifs, borders, and photo mats). It is best to use straight-edged scissors; unless decorative-edged scissors are extremely sharp, cutting fabric is difficult. Peel off the paper backing, place it onto the background page as desired, and iron in place according to manufacturer's directions. Trim around the outside edges of the background page if excess fabric, fibers, or fusible web extend off the page.

3 Once the photos have been cropped to the desired shapes and sizes, adhere them directly to the background pages, fabric-covered background pages, fabric photo mats, or to card stock for matting. As desired, the photos can be single- or double-matted and trimmed with decorative-edged scissors.

1 Using acrylic paint, base-paint the background page with light tan. Using an old toothbrush, spatter it with light brown for an aged look.

2 Using fabric motifs or borders as mats will help offset any photo. As shown above, iron the fabric border down the right-hand side of the background page and the fabric photo mats to the center of the page.

3 Using an appropriate adhesive, adhere the photos in place.

BASIC SUPPLIES: Adhesive; assortment of solid and patterned fabrics, felts, ribbons and trims; fusible web; iron and ironing board; journaling pen or marker; photos; scissors; purchased scrapbook album with pages included; photo cropping templates

ADDITIONAL SUPPLIES: Embroidery floss; fine-point markers; paintbrushes; acrylic paints; decorative-edged scissors; sponge; assortment of stickers or card stock; stylus; old toothbrush

1 Using acrylic paint, base-paint the background page with navy blue. Using an old toothbrush, spatter it with white for a wintery look.

2 Iron a small fabric border across the top of the background page.

3 Using fusible web, appliqué the snowman pieces except for the heart. Using embroidery floss, tie the heart to the mittens, then iron in place. Using three strands of orange embroidery floss, stitch the carrot nose. Using a fine-point black marker, dot the eyes and mouth. Iron the snowman in place at the bottom of the background page.

4 Using decorative-edged scissors, cut the photos into circles for "snowballs." Using an appropriate adhesive, adhere the photos in place.

5 Add painted white lines around the snowballs to create the illusion of movement.

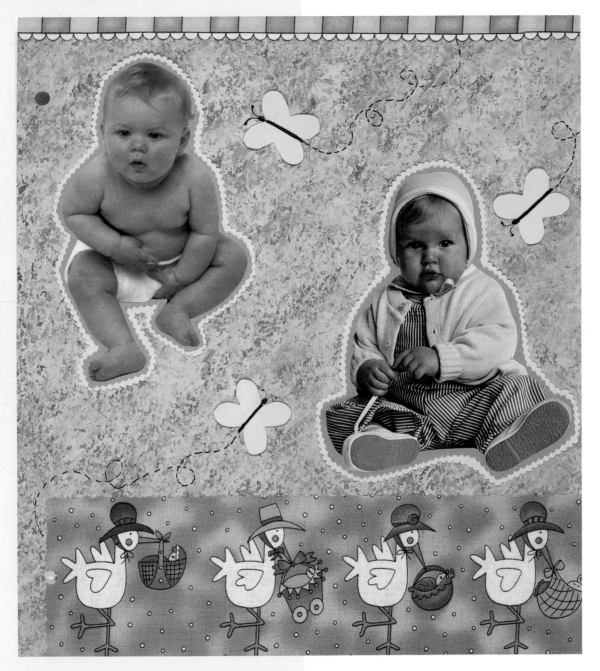

1 Using acrylic paint, base-paint the background page with royal blue. Sponge it with dusty blue for a variegated look.

2 Iron a small fabric border across the top of the background page and a larger fabric border across the bottom.

3 As shown above, silhouette the photos.

4 As desired, the photos can be single- or double-matted and trimmed with decorative-edged scissors.

5 Using an appropriate adhesive, adhere the photos in place.

6 Randomly add hand-cut butterflies or butterfly stickers around the photos. Using a fine-point black marker, draw the "butterfly trails."

1 Using acrylic paints and a stylus, randomly add "dots" on the background page with several colors.

2 Iron the fabric border down the right-hand side of the background page.

3 As shown above, silhouette the photo(s).

4 As desired, the photo(s) can be single- or double-matted and trimmed with decorative-edged scissors.

5 Using an appropriate adhesive, adhere the photo(s) in place.

1 Iron fabric to cover the entire background page.

2 Add three strips of coordinating ribbon across the top of the page.

3 Cut three oak leaves and one acorn from contrasting fabrics. Overlap the leaves and acorns as desired and iron in place at the bottom right-hand corner of the background page. Using a fine-point black marker, draw veins in the oak leaves and accent lines around the acorn.

4 As desired, the photos can be single- or double-matted and trimmed with decorative-edged scissors.

5 Using an appropriate adhesive, adhere the photos in place.

1 Using acrylic paint, base-paint the background page with off-white. Using an old toothbrush, spatter it with russet for an autumnal look.

2 Cut eight oak leaves and six acorns from contrasting fabrics. Overlap the leaves and acorns as desired and iron in place down the right-hand side of the background page. Using a fine-point black marker, draw veins in the oak leaves and accent lines around the acorns. As shown at left, draw stitch lines around the leaves and acorns to accentuate the designs.

3 As desired, the photo(s) can be single- or double-matted and trimmed with decorative-edged scissors.

4 Using an appropriate adhesive, adhere the photo(s) in place.

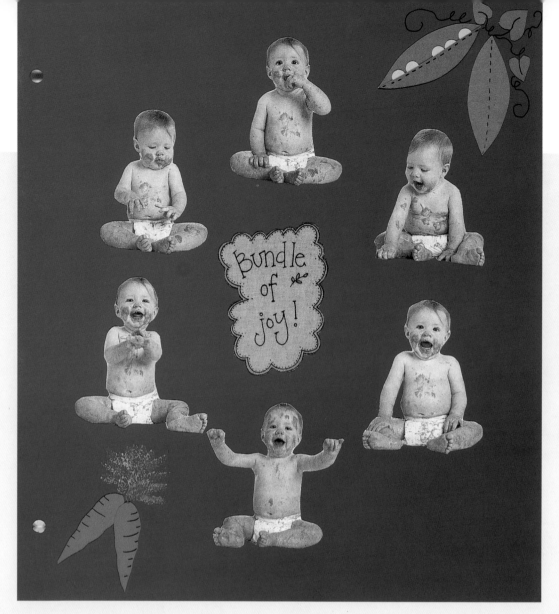

1 Using acrylic paint, base-paint the background page with dark country blue.

2 Iron a fabric motif in the center of the background page.

3 As shown above, silhouette the photos.

4 Using an appropriate adhesive, adhere the photos in a circle around the fabric motif.

5 Add hand-cut peas and carrots or peas and carrot stickers in opposite corners of the back-

ground page. If using hand-cut carrots, sponge the tops directly onto the background page. Using a fine-point marker, draw accent marks on the peas and carrots and draw a vine connecting the pea pods and leaves.

6 As desired, the photo(s) can be single- or double-matted and trimmed with decorative-edged scissors.

7 Using an appropriate adhesive, adhere the photo(s) in place.

EMBELLISHING & BINDING THE COVER

Disassemble a purchased scrapbook album. Cut a piece of fabric and a piece of cotton batting to the dimensions necessary to cover the album, allowing at least one inch on all sides for folding over to the inside of the album. Pin the piece of cotton batting to the wrong side of the fabric. Using a sewing machine and thread to complement the fabric, stitch horizontal and vertical lines to quilt the fabric. Place the quilted fabric, right side down, on a clean, flat surface that has been covered with waxed paper to protect it.

Using a 1/2" flat paintbrush, apply an appropriate adhesive or découpage medium over the outside cover of the album. It may be necessary to do this one section at a time. Center the album over the quilted fabric and press down to remove air pockets. Bring the edges of the quilted fabric around to the inside of the album cover and adhere. To reduce bulk, clip and miter the corners. Let the adhesive or découpage medium dry thoroughly.

Cut two pieces of fabric to the dimensions necessary to cover the inside of the album, less one-quarter inch all sides. Adhere these pieces of fabric to the inside of the album cover to hide the raw edges of the quilted fabric.

To embellish the front of the album, copy the saying onto color copy transfer paper. Make certain the copy is made in mirror image.

Using fusible web, attach a piece of muslin to a piece of cotton batting. Iron the color copied saying onto the fused fabric. Cut the fused fabric into the shape of a heart around the saying.

Using an embroidery needle and six strands of embroidery floss, sew a running stitch around the outside perimeter of the heart and tie a bow at the top of the heart. Cut off excess embroidery floss and tie a knot at each loose end. Adhere the fused fabric heart to the front of the album as desired.

The album shown has an expandable post binding. Place the completed scrapbook pages in the desired order and place them inside the album cover. Reassemble the purchased scrapbook album.

Photo shown on page 100.

SUPPLIES FOR EMBELLISHING THE COVER: Adhesive; cotton batting; embroidery floss; embroidery needle; patterned fabrics; fusible web; iron and ironing board; a piece of muslin; 1/2" flat paintbrush; scissors; purchased scrapbook album with pages included; sewing machine and thread; straight pins; color copy transfer paper; waxed paper

HAVEN

FAMILY

HOME SWEET HOME

Home is where the heart is

COMFORT

"MAY A WELCOMING WARMTH ALWAYS BURN IN YOUR HEARTH,
AND THE VIEW FROM YOUR WINDOW BRING JOY TO YOUR HEART."
— AUTHOR UNKNOWN

USING FAUX FINISHES

1 Choose solid card stock to be used as the background pages.

2 There are several faux-finish techniques that can be used to create incredible background pages. Each background page can be created individually or one "master" page can be created and color-copied for the remaining album pages.

3 Each of the techniques described are unique and diverse. Create the various faux finishes according to manufacturer's directions.

4 Once the photos have been cropped to the desired shapes and sizes, adhere them directly to the background pages or to card stock for matting. As desired, the photos can be single- or double-matted and trimmed with decorative-edged scissors.

BASIC SUPPLIES: Adhesive; antiquing medium; bristle brush; sponge brush; sponge pouncing brush or sea sponge; liner brush; soft cloth; crackle medium; crackle medium activator; craft knife; cutting mat; eraser; gold foil; gold foil adhesive; glazing medium; fine-point black marker; masking fluid; flat paintbrushes; acrylic paints; textured acrylic paints; disposable palette; journaling pen or marker; pencil; photos; rubbing alcohol; ruler; scissors; purchased scrapbook album with pages included; splashing tool or bristle brush; spray bottle; table salt; low tack tape; masking tape; decorative-edged template; photo cropping templates; waterbase varnish

ADDITIONAL SUPPLIES: Embossing fluid pen; embossing powder; heat tool; 140 lb. cold-pressed watercolor paper; decorative-edged scissors

"THE HOME SHOULD BE A HAVEN ...
A PLACE OF REFUGE, A PLACE OF PEACE,
A PLACE OF HARMONY, A PLACE OF BEAUTY."
— MARY C. CROWLEY

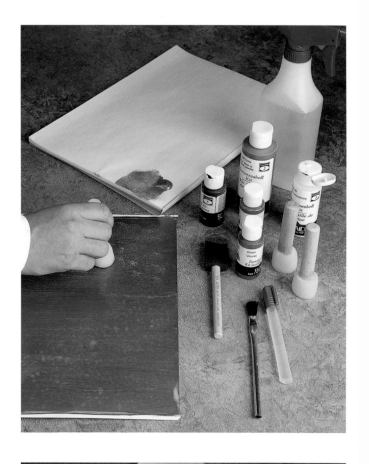

1 Before you begin, make certain your scrapbook album cover or background pages are clean and free of debris. Read all directions and proceed according to manufacturer's directions.

2 Remove the cap and tip from the splashing tool. Using a funnel, fill the splashing tool with rubbing alcohol. Replace the cap and tip.

3 Using a sponge brush, paint the background page with antique metallic gold acrylic paint. Apply a second coat of the acrylic paint. If necessary, apply a third coat of the acrylic paint. Let the acrylic paint dry thoroughly between each coat.

Brush a coat of clear glazing medium over the background page. Do not let it dry; to achieve the tortoiseshell technique it is important that you work wet on wet. The glazing medium needs to be moist but not runny. Keep a spray bottle of water available to mist the background page if it starts to dry.

Using a sponge pouncing brush or wet sea sponge that has been wrung out to remove any excess water, dip the brush (sponge) into the metallic gold acrylic paint. Pounce the sponge on a disposable palette to remove excess acrylic paint, then randomly pounce over the painted background page. Make certain you can still see the base color. Repeat process with copper, then black acrylic paints. Be careful not to overwork or the appearance will be muddy; it is important that you can see all of the colors.

Using the spray bottle, mist the background page with water. Using the splashing tool or a bristle brush, spatter the page with the alcohol. You should immediately see a reaction from the acrylic paints. Let the water and the alcohol dry thoroughly.

If there are harsh edges on the circles, use a bristle brush to eliminate them. Wait about five to ten minutes, then splash again with more alcohol.

"THE VOYAGE OF DISCOVERY
IS NOT IN SEEKING
NEW LANDSCAPES,
BUT IN HAVING NEW EYES."
— MARCEL PROUST

1 Using a sponge brush, paint the background page with antique metallic gold acrylic paint. Apply a second coat of the acrylic paint. Let the acrylic paint dry thoroughly between each coat.

2 Brush a coat of clear glazing medium over the background page. Do not let it dry; to achieve the tortoiseshell technique it is important that you work wet on wet. The glazing medium needs to be moist but not runny. Keep a spray bottle of water available to mist the background page if it starts to dry.

3 Using a wet sea sponge that has been wrung out to remove any excess water, dip the sponge into the metallic gold acrylic paint. Pounce the sponge on a disposable palette to remove excess paint, then randomly pounce over the painted background page. Make certain you can still see the base color. Repeat process with copper, then black acrylic paints. Be careful not to overwork or the appearance will be muddy; it is important that you can see all of the colors.

4 Using the spray bottle, mist the background page with water. Using a bristle brush, spatter the page with rubbing alcohol. You should immediately see a reaction from the acrylic paints. Let the water and the alcohol dry thoroughly.

5 Transfer the photo frame to the background page. Using an embossing fluid pen, outline the photo frame. Generously cover the embossing fluid with gold embossing powder; then remove any excess embossing powder (do not discard it as it can be reused). Using a heat tool, emboss the photo frame.

6 Using an appropriate adhesive, adhere the photos in place on the background page as desired.

Shown on page 114.

1 Pour a small amount of dark green and avocado green acrylic paints onto a disposable palette. Add enough water to thin each color to an inky (watercolor) consistency and set aside.

2 Using a sponge brush, wet the background page with water until it looks shiny. Randomly apply spots of the green washes on the background page until the colors run together and the page is completely covered.

3 Sprinkle table salt over the background page and set aside.

4 Once the background page is thoroughly dry, brush off the table salt.

5 Using masking tape, mask off a border on the background page as desired. Paint inside the border with dark green acrylic paint. Let the acrylic paint dry thoroughly.

6 Apply crackle medium to the painted border according to manufacturer's directions.

7 Paint the painted border with avocado green acrylic paint. Let the acrylic paint dry thoroughly.

8 Apply crackle medium activator to the painted border according to manufacturer's directions. The cracks will appear as the crackle medium activator dries. Remove the masking tape.

9 Using an appropriate adhesive, adhere the photos in place on the background page as desired.

1 Using masking tape, mask off a border on the background page as desired. Paint inside the border with black green acrylic paint. Let the acrylic paint dry thoroughly. Apply a second coat of the black green acrylic paint.

2 Pour a small amount of colonial green acrylic paint onto a disposable palette. Using a wet sea sponge that has been wrung out to remove any excess water, dip sponge into the acrylic paint. Pounce the sponge on the disposable palette to remove excess acrylic paint, then randomly pounce over the painted border. Repeat

process with metallic gold acrylic paint. Remove the masking tape.

3 Using an appropriate adhesive, adhere the photos in place on the background page as desired.

4 To make additional motifs, repeat process as with decorative border on 140 lb. cold-pressed watercolor paper. There is no need to mask off any design. Once the application is dry, simply cut the motifs from the watercolor paper and adhere in place as desired.

Home...

1 Using a liner brush and masking fluid, write sayings about the subject you are scrapbooking. In this case, about the home. Let the masking fluid dry thoroughly.

2 Using acrylic paint, paint the entire background page with turquoise. Let the acrylic paint dry thoroughly.

3 Using masking tape, mask off a wide border on the background page as desired. You will want to mask the area that you have written in. Using a wet sea sponge that has been wrung out to remove any excess water, dip sponge into metallic bronze acrylic paint. Pounce the sponge on a disposable palette to remove excess acrylic paint, then randomly pounce over the painted background page, within the masked off border only. Make certain you can still see the base color. Repeat process with copper.

4 Remove the masking fluid by rubbing over the painted area with your finger or it can be erased with an eraser. Using a fine-point black marker, very loosely write sayings over the white writing as shown above. Remove the masking tape.

5 Using a flat paintbrush, paint a word that best describes your overall subject matter. In this case, the word "Home." Use thin and thick strokes. Outline the bottoms and to the left of each letter with a contrasting color.

6 Using an appropriate adhesive, adhere the photos in place on the background page as desired.

1 Measure ½" in from the right-hand side of the background page and lightly draw a pencil line. Place a piece of low tack tape above the pencil line, then place one or two more pieces of the tape below the first piece of tape. Make certain the pieces of tape are flush with each other and go directly beneath each other.

2 Using a decorative-edged template, trace the pattern of the template on the top of the bottom section of tape. Trace over the line with a sharp craft knife and remove the center portion of the tape to reveal the pattern. Do not disturb the remaining pieces of tape.

3 Using a sponge brush, apply one coat of pure gold acrylic paint between the pieces of tape. Let the acrylic paint dry thoroughly.

4 Pounce a bristle brush in gold foil adhesive, then pounce the brush over the painted gold area. Let the gold foil adhesive dry thoroughly.

5 Apply the gold foil, dull-side down, over the gold foil adhesive and rub it with your fingers. Remove the gold foil sheet.

6 Using a sponge brush, apply antiquing medium over the gold foiled area. Using a soft cloth, wipe off excess antiquing medium. Let antiquing medium dry thoroughly. Remove the low tack tape.

7 Using an appropriate adhesive, adhere the photos in place on the background page as desired.

8 To make photo corners, repeat process as with decorative border on 140 lb. cold-pressed watercolor paper. There is no need to mask off any design. Once the application is dry, simply cut the photo corners from the watercolor paper and adhere in place at the corners of each desired photo.

1 Using masking tape, mask approximately 1" to 1¹/₂" off the right-hand side of the background page.

2 Pour stone-like textured acrylic paint onto a disposable palette. Using a sponge brush, apply a generous amount of the textured paint to the background page to the right of the masking tape. Let the textured paint dry thoroughly.

3 Using a sponge brush, apply one coat of waterbase varnish over the textured paint. Let the varnish dry thoroughly.

4 Mix one part black acrylic paint to one part glazing medium. Using a damp sea sponge, apply the black glazing mixture over the textured area on the background page. Make certain the glazing mixture gets into the crevices, but don't use too much of the black glazing mixture. Let the glazing mixture dry thoroughly.

5 Mix one part avocado green acrylic paint to one part glazing medium. Using a damp sea sponge, pounce the avocado green glazing mixture randomly over the black. Let the glazing mixture dry thoroughly.

6 Using a sponge brush, apply one coat of waterbase varnish over the painted textured paint. Let the varnish dry thoroughly. Remove the masking tape.

7 Using an appropriate adhesive, adhere the photos in place on the background page as desired.

EMBELLISHING & BINDING THE COVER

1 Disassemble a purchased scrapbook album. Using a sponge brush and acrylic paint, paint the front and back covers of the album (inside and out) with two to three coats of golden brown. Let the acrylic paint dry thoroughly between each coat.

2 Mix one part dark brown acrylic paint to one part glazing medium. Using a sponge, apply the glazing mixture to the album cover.

3 Dampen a chamois leather tool with water. Squeeze out any excess water and pounce it on the album cover over the glazing mixture. Let the glazing mixture dry thoroughly.

4 Using additional colors of acrylic paint, paint a decorative border around the edges of the front cover and write a phrase in the center.

5 Using an old toothbrush, spatter the front cover of the scrapbook album.

6 Place the completed scrapbook pages in the desired order and place them inside the album cover. Reassemble the purchased scrapbook album.

Photo shown on page 108.

SUPPLIES FOR EMBELLISHING THE COVER:

Chamois leather tool; sponge brush; glazing medium; acrylic paints; purchased scrapbook album with pages included; sponge

"ONE HUNDRED YEARS FROM NOW,
IT WILL NOT MATTER WHAT KIND OF CAR I DROVE,
WHAT KIND OF HOUSE I LIVED IN
OR HOW MUCH MONEY I HAD IN THE BANK,
BUT THE WORLD MAY BE A BETTER PLACE
BECAUSE I MADE A DIFFERENCE
IN A CHILD'S LIFE."
— AUTHOR UNKNOWN

USING STICKERS

1 Choose solid papers to be used as the background pages. Using an appropriate adhesive, adhere the background pages to the album pages. In all of the sample pages shown, the stickers were placed directly on the album pages.

2 Carefully arrange the stickers on the background page as desired without applying too much pressure to each sticker. This makes it simple to remove the sticker for repositioning when necessary. Once the design is in place, rub each sticker down onto the background page with clean hands. If stickers need to be removed permanently or tem-porarily for repositioning, a commercial adhesive stabilizer can be used so that no damage is done to the background page or to other stickers that have been used. Once the sticker has been removed, it can be re-used by repositioning it and rubbing it down into its new position.

3 Once the photos have been cropped to the desired shapes and sizes, adhere them directly to the background pages or to card stock for matting. As desired, the photos can be single- or double-matted and trimmed with decorative-edged scissors.

BASIC SUPPLIES: Adhesive; adhesive stabilizer; craft knife; cutting mat; fine- and medium-point markers; assortment of solid papers; journaling pen or marker; photos; scissors; decorative-edged scissors; purchased scrapbook album with pages included; assortment of stickers; photo cropping templates

> "PEACE IS NOT SOMETHING YOU WISH FOR;
> IT IS SOMETHING YOU MAKE,
> SOMETHING YOU DO,
> SOMETHING YOU ARE,
> AND SOMETHING YOU GIVE AWAY."
> — ROBERT FULGHUM

1 Using a fine-point marker, draw a border around the perimeter of the background page to be used for positioning the small flower stickers.

2 Place a cluster of larger flower stickers in the bottom corners of the background page. Overlapping is essential to get this type of effect.

THE APPLE OF

1 Using stripe stickers, make a decorative border down the right-hand side of the background page and a horizontal line across the bottom.

2 As shown above, alphabet stickers in two different colors are used. When using alphabet or number stickers, make them "crooked" for a more interesting look. This is much simpler than trying to get each letter straight and perfectly spaced.

3 Using scallop-edged scissors, cut a "bite" from one of the apple stickers.

OUR EYE

WHAT A TWEETHEART!

1 Using basic geometric-shaped stickers, create the birdhouses and flowers by layering the stickers.

2 As shown above, each birdhouse was created using one triangle (roof), one square (house) and one circle (opening).

3 One flower was created with five hearts (petals), one circle (inside of flower), and one circle, cut into quarters (leaves). Two other flowers were created with circles from which a small wedge was removed. Again, the leaves are portions of circles. The third type of flower was created with two hearts (petals), a wedge-shaped section of a circle, and one heart, cut in half (leaves). All of the birdhouse poles and flower stems are stripe stickers.

1 Using a sharp craft knife, trim the stickers as necessary so they appear to be ending at or "falling off" the edge of the background page.

2 As shown above, placing stickers on top of die-cut letters and overlapping onto more than one letter is a unique way to tie in any theme.

1 Using a medium-point marker, draw a border around the two outside edges of two facing background pages to be used for positioning the leaf and ladybug stickers. When placed together, a double-page spread is created, allowing the use of several photos.

2 Randomly place additional stickers with a gardening theme alongside the border of one or both pages as desired.

3 Using a fine-point marker, draw the "ladybug trails."

"LIFE IS FOR JOY, FOR GIVING, FOR SHARING, AND FOR LAUGHTER. BUT MOSTLY, IT IS FOR LOVE."
— AUTHOR UNKNOWN